MW01052908

Harry Teel's No Nonsense

Guide To Fly Fishing

In Central & Southeastern Oregon

Published by David Communications ● 6171 Tollgate, Sisters, Oregon 97759

Preface

I'm very fortunate in many ways. But as this fortune relates to fly fishing, I'm fortunate that I was born in Oregon, and fortunate that I was introduced to fly fishing by my father and his friends at a very early age. These circumstances have allowed me to pursue trout, steelhead and salmon fishing nearly continuously for the better part of sixty years.

Fly fishing has been an important part of these sixty-plus years, both as a form of recreation and as a business. There have been only two interruptions in my quest for full-time fishing however. The first was my tour of duty in the South Pacific and China with the Marine Corp during W.W.II. The other when I worked for thirty years with CH2M Hill, Engineers. The latter was much more enjoyable than my first diversion from fly fishing. It also enabled me to support my wife and five robin-mouthed offspring. These working years also provided me the opportunity to work in close association with the finest professional and technical people in engineering.

After retiring from CH2M Hill, and finding retirement somewhat boring, I opened The Fly Fishers Place, a fly shop in the Central Oregon town of Sisters. Running the shop was a most interesting, enjoyable and rewarding experience. It's allowed me to meet hundreds of wonderful people, fish with new friends, travel, explore fishing opportunities in other locations, and fulfill my lifelong dream of being involved in fly fishing on a full-time basis. I've also been able to record my fly fishing adventures in Oregon and now, through this guide, can offer you the benefit of these years of fly fishing and note-taking.

The Central and Southeast regions of Oregon, (High Desert region) are the origins of some of the most beautiful and pristine lakes and streams to be found anywhere in the world. Each region has its own distinct character and splendor. Some waters are bounded by old-growth forests of pine and fir, while others are surrounded by ancient junipers and desert vegetation.

When you're casting your fly to a rising trout, it is at times difficult to keep your concentration on fishing when the vistas beyond your quarry are the snow-covered peaks of the Cascade Mountains, the desert's wonderful rimrock canyons or the sheer magnitude of the Steens Mountain. The scenery is a photographers dream and a fly anglers haven.

The Central and Southeast regions also offer many opportunities for solitude. In most areas a short walk will take you into territory that is nearly undisturbed by human endeavors. Taking a break in the high desert country is a wonderful way to relax and rejuvenate your mind and body.

I believe you'll enjoy the fly fishing in this magnificent part of Oregon. More importantly, I think your fly fishing experiences in this area will always occupy a special place in your memory.

Acknowledgments

For this fourth edition, people suggested I include new waters. Some I've not fished, but I know to be of merit. I asked Jeff Perin, owner of The Fly Fisher's Place in Sisters, Oregon, if he would be kind enough to research these areas for inclusion in this guidebook. He agreed. Jeff's name is noted in sections where he provided input and updated information. His valuable contributions to this edition include new lakes, charts and information on steelhead fishing on the lower Deschutes.

Harry Teel

Harry Teel's No Nonsense
Guide To Fly Fishing Central and Southeastern Oregon

©1998 David Communications
ISBN #0-9637256-9-6
New, Updated & Improved 5th Printing
Published by
David Communications
6171 Tollgate • Sisters, Oregon 97759

Author: Harry Teel *Input:* Jeff Perin
Maps & Illustrations: Harry Teel, Pete Chadwell
Proofing: Harry Teel, Adrienne Banks

Production & Art Direction: Aprille Chadwell
Editor: David Banks
Cover Photos: Brad Teel, David Banks

David Communications believes that in addition to No Nonsense, local information and gear, fly fishers need fresh water and healthy fish. The publisher encourages preservation, improvement, conservation, enjoyment and understanding of our waters and their inhabitants. A good way to do this is to support organizations dedicated to these ideas.

David Communications is a member, sponsor and donor to Trout Unlimited, The Federation of Fly Fishers, Oregon Trout, California Trout, New Mexico Trout, Amigos Bravos, American Fly Tackle Trade Association, American Rivers, Waterfowl U.S.A. and Ducks Unlimited. We encourage you to get involved, learn more and to join such organizations.

• Trout Unlimited 1(800) 834-2419 • Federation of Fly Fishers (406) 585-7592 • Oregon Trout (503) 222-9091 •
• California Trout (415) 392-8887 • Waterfowl U.S.A. • New Mexico Trout (505) 344-6363 •
• Amigos Bravos (505) 758-3874 • American Rivers (202) 547-6900 • Ducks Unlimited: (901) 758-3825 •

*T*his guide is dedicated to my wife, Delores, and my five children, Brad, Bruce, Susan, Brett and Shelley. Under duress at times, they've accompanied me on numerous fishing excursions and . . . . To my many fishing friends who have taught me the fine points of reading water, casting, selecting flies, the necessity of good equipment and how to camp in perfect misery on a beautiful, warm summer day.

VICINITY MAP

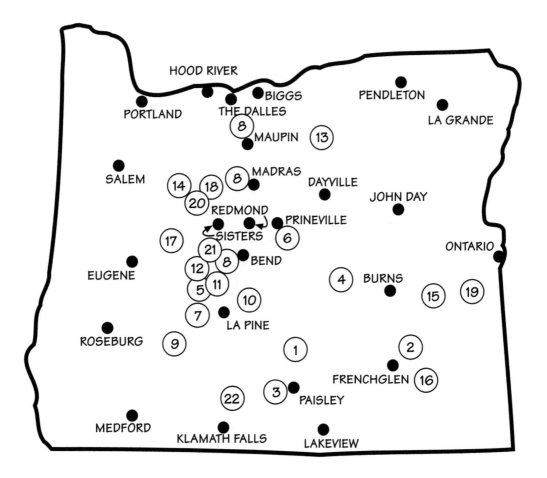

REFERENCED STREAMS, LAKES AND RESERVOIRS

1. ANA RIVER
2. BLITZEN RIVER
3. CHEWAUCAN RIVER
4. CHICKAHOMINY RESERVOIR
5. CRANE PRAIRIE RESERVOIR
6. CROOKED RIVER
7. DAVIS LAKE
8. DESCHUTES RIVER
9. DIAMOND LAKE
10. EAST LAKE
11. FALL RIVER

12. HOSMER LAKE
13. JOHN DAY RIVER
14. LOST LAKE
15. MALHEUR RIVER
16. MANN LAKE
17. McKENZIE RIVER
18. METOLIUS RIVER
19. OWYHEE RIVER
20. SUTTLE LAKE
21. THREE CREEKS LAKE
22. WILLIAMSON RIVER

Contents

Top Central and Southeastern Oregon Fly Fishing Waters

Appendix

Introduction

Thoughts on the State, Conservation and the Future

My first experience on a fishing trip to Central Oregon was with my father in 1933. At that time we lived in Milwaukie, Oregon, which is southeast of Portland. While visiting a neighbor, we were shown large rainbow trout he'd recently caught in the Deschutes River. The image is still vivid, even though it was some sixty-five years ago when I was a boy of six. The following Sunday Dad got me up at 3:00 AM. We jumped in the pickup and headed for Maupin, a small community on the banks of the Deschutes about 100 miles east of home. I followed Dad up and down the river that day. When he hooked a fish he'd let me land it, or at least try. We didn't end up with the number or size of trout that we'd seen at our neighbors, but it was a memorable day. It provided me with a lasting memory of my Dad and it was the day I started my continuing love for the Deschutes River and the Central and Southeast regions of Oregon.

Since that first experience on the Deschutes River, I've fished the High Desert regions of Oregon hundreds of times. I've also had the good fortune to have fly fished from Argentina to Alaska. This has included the San Juan River in New Mexico, the Green River in Utah, the Wood in Idaho, and the Madison, Ruby and Beaverhead in Montana. But, if the truth be known, Central and Southeast Oregon compares favorably, and in many cases exceeds the fly fishing I found in most other parts of the lower forty-eight states.

Fishing lakes and reservoirs is a whole different program than fishing streams. On streams, it's relatively easy to read the water and determine the feeding lanes and holds. That's not true with the still water of lakes. The surface is flat without a lot of indicators to tell you where to fish. Look at the shore line, identify submerged objects, study contour maps of the bottom, scan for surface activity and observe where other people are fishing. You may need to keep moving and exploring until you find where the fish are active. This active spot can change from hour to hour.

To give you an example of what I'm talking about, I once had a banner day fishing Davis Lake. I fished the main lake, near the O'Dell Creek channel, with a small Adams pattern. (Fishing dry flies for Davis fish always excites me.) Two days later I took my son Brad to this hot spot.

There were about eight other boats in the vicinity which seemed to indicate that the fish were still working the area. We anchored and started fishing, while observing what kind of success other people were having.

After about 45 minutes we hadn't a rise and saw only one other fish taken. I switched to a nymph with the same results: nothing. About this time, we noted several fish working the reed beds almost into the channel. We pulled anchor and headed towards the rising fish. We positioned the boat, anchored, switched to dry patterns and started casting towards the reeds. The first cast produced a rise, but no fish.

That was the last fish we'd see coming to a dry pattern. We didn't do anything with Montanas or Leeches either. We then moved well into the channel just before calling it a day.

On the way in I put on a Prince nymph and cast towards the reeds. After several casts I hooked a nice fish. We anchored. Over the next hour we enjoyed catching and releasing a dozen Rainbows from 13" to 20". This was just a case of observing, moving, changing patterns and plain old fisherman's luck.

The message I convey is: don't get too enamored with what happened yesterday or that morning, but concentrate on finding the fish when you're on the water. There are times when you'll need all your skill and luck to accomplish this.

A word of advice. Always get information. No matter where you're going fly fishing, there is a right time to be there, a right technique and a right fly pattern. Ask someone or check reputable literature (like this guide). Your best bet, in many cases, is to call a fly shop in the region. Several good ones are listed in the back of this guide. If you're still not getting the information you need, you can call me in Bend, Oregon. My telephone number is in the book.

A word on words. Like it says on the cover, this is a "no nonsense" guide. I've tried to eliminate a lot of small talk, flowery adjectives and unimportant folderol. This is an easy reading guide with essential and basic information. It will help you decide what water to visit and give you what you'll need to know to have a good time fly fishing.

When you're fishing Central and Southeast Oregon rivers, streams, lakes and reservoirs (or any place, for that matter) please practice conservation. Catch and release is a good way to start. And consider the five guidelines that all conscientious fly fishers obey:

- Abide by the laws.
- Respect property owners rights.
- Be considerate of others.
- Never crowd in on another fisher.
- Carry out your litter.

Central Oregon Fly Fishing Brief

The basic features of fly fishing Oregon's popular High Desert region

*I*n the Central and Southeast regions of Oregon, there are hundreds of lakes and reservoirs and miles and miles of rivers and creeks. I've not included all of these waters in this guide, but rather those that I've fished with success and those that are readily accessible to the public. I've also included comments on eight private (with a fee) lakes, but only because Jeff and I feel they're worth the price of admission.

A word on the ratings. Each river, stream, lake and reservoir in the main section of this guide has been rated on a scale from one to ten. A "ten" is water that offers the best possible fly fishing experience Oregon has to offer. A "one" would be fishable, but not much else.

These ratings are based on my experience fly fishing these waters over a number of years. Thus, my rating may not necessarily coincide with the experience you had on your particular day fly fishing, or even your combined experience. The best uses of these ratings are as a way to get a general idea of a particular fly fishing destination and as a means of comparing our opinions.

Here are the basics you should scan and know before deciding what water to go fly fish.

Gamefish
Rainbow, brown, cutthroat, brook trout, steelhead and bull trout are found throughout Central Oregon. Other species include kokanee salmon, bass and a variety of panfish.

Catch & Release
Many Oregon waters have limited-kill regulations. Responsible anglers practice catch and release and are careful handling fish.

Weather
High desert weather can be warm and ideal or very, very cold and windy. Weather in the Cascade mountains can change quickly from comfortable to rain, wind or snow. Be prepared for extreme weather in this region any time of year.

Hazards & Safety
Use a wading staff in rivers like the Deschutes and other big streams that have fast currents and rocky bottoms.

Don't drink the water unless you've purified it. Unfortunately, giardia is common enough.

Use caution with fires when camping. Always tell someone where you are going and when you expect to return.

Rods
An all-around rod is a 9 foot 5 weight. You can fish most waters in this guidebook with this size and weight. For small creeks try a 7 foot 3 weight rod. Float tubers prefer 9 1/2-10 foot rods.

Reels
Palm, click or disc drags work fine for most Central Oregon fly waters. About 75 yards of backing is usually adequate for trout. You'll need more for steelhead.

Lines & Leaders
A floating line can be used for most all streams and stillwaters in our region. Occasionally a sink tip or sinking line is an advantage. Some lakes and reservoirs fish better with a type 2 fast sinking and an intermediate sinking line.

Leaders should be stout for sinking lines, 2x-4x. For dries and nymphing, 9-12 foot leaders, 4x-6x are about right.

Wading Gear
I suggest felt-soled wading boots and a wading staff for most every water in the region. A wading staff and cleats are helpful and recommend while fly fishing in the Deschutes. Wet wading is possible during the summer months, especially in the eastern part of the state. Float tubers need neoprene chest-high waders and warm clothes. Mountain waters are c-o-l-d.

Guides
If you are new to the sport, or to Oregon, a days outing with a qualified guide will help you learn the ropes. Check with the fly shops in the back of this guidebook for waters that permit guided fly fishing.

Private Fly Fishing Waters
Paying for a day or two on a private water can be rewarding. If you are a fly fishing novice, private waters offer a great way to hone your skills. The private waters listed towards the back of this guidebook can offer excellent fishing in remote or isolated locations. They are a good value and worth your consideration.

Trash
Leaving an area better than you found it is the responsibility of all fly fishers. But enough of the obvious stuff. Here's hoping you hook that fish you've always dreamed of on one of the waters in this guide.

Fly Fishing Conditions By The Month

H ere are general fly fishing conditions for Central and Southeast Oregon. Use this list to help plan your fly fishing outing or vacation. Water conditons can vary from year to year as can seasons and regulations. This can affect these conditions. Always consult a fly shop to get the latest information.

KEY: **P** = Prime, best fly fishing.   **G** = Good, OK fly fishing.
F = Fair, fishable but inconsistent. **NF** = Not fishable or closed.

	Jan	Feb	Mar	April	May	June	July	Aug	Sept	Oct	Nov	Dec
Ana Reservoir	F	G	G	F	F	F	F	F	G	G	G	F
Ana River	F	F	F	F	P	P	F	F	P	P	F	F
Antelope Reservoir	NF	NF	G	G	F	F	G	G	P	G	G	NF
Big Indian Creek	NF	NF	NF	NF	F	F	G	G	G	G	F	F
Blitzen River	NF	NF	NF	NF	NF	F	P	P	P	P	NF	NF
Chewaucan River	NF	NF	NF	F	F	G	G	P	P	G	F	F
Chickahominy Res.	NF	NF	P	P	G	F	F	F	F	P	P	NF
Crane Prairie Res.	NF	NF	NF	F	F	P	P	P	P	G	NF	NF
Crescent Creek	NF	NF	NF	F	F	F	G	G	G	G	NF	NF
Crooked River	F	F	G	G	F	F	P	P	P	G	G	F
Davis Lake	NF	NF	F	G	P	P	P	P	P	F	F	NF
Deep Creek	NF	NF	NF	F	F	G	P	P	P	G	F	F
Delintment Lake	NF	NF	NF	F	G	G	G	G	G	F	F	F
Deschutes River	F	F	F	G	P	P	P	P	P	P	F	F
Little Deschutes R.	NF	NF	NF	F	F	F	G	G	G	G	NF	NF
Diamond Lake	NF	NF	NF	G	G	P	P	P	P	P	NF	NF
Duncan Reservoir	NF	NF	NF	F	F	G	G	G	G	G	F	F
East Lake	NF	NF	NF	F	G	P	P	P	P	G	NF	NF
Fall River	G	G	G	G	G	P	P	P	P	G	G	F
Fish Lake	NF	NF	NF	NF	NF	F	P	P	P	F	F	NF
Hosmer Lake	NF	NF	NF	F	F	G	G	G	G	G	F	NF
John Day River	F	F	F	F	G	G	G	G	G	G	G	F
Krumbo Reservoir	NF	NF	NF	F	F	G	G	G	G	G	F	F
Lost Lake	NF	NF	NF	F	G	G	G	F	F	G	NF	NF
Malheur River	F	F	G	G	F	F	F	F	F	P	P	F
Mann Lake	NF	NF	F	F	F	G	P	P	P	P	F	NF
McKenzie River*	NF	NF	NF	F	P	P	P	P	P	F	NF	NF
Metolius River	F	F	F	F	P	P	P	P	P	F	F	F
Owyhee River	F	G	F	F	G	G	G	G	P	P	G	F
Powder River	NF	NF	NF	F	G	G	G	G	P	P	F	F
Round, Square, Long,	NF	NF	NF	NF	F	P	G	G	P	F	NF	NF
Meadow Lakes	NF	NF	NF	NF	F	P	G	G	P	F	NF	NF
Suttle Lake	NF	NF	NF	NF	F	F	G	G	P	P	NF	NF
Thompson Reservoir	NF	NF	NF	G	G	G	G	P	P	P	F	NF
Three Creeks Lake	NF	NF	NF	NF	NF	G	P	P	P	G	NF	NF
Wickiup Reservoir	NF	NF	NF	F	G	P	P	P	P	P	NF	NF
Williamson River	NF	NF	NF	NF	G	G	G	G	G	G	NF	NF
Yellow Jacket Lake	NF	NF	NF	F	F	G	P	P	P	G	NF	NF

* Denotes upper river. Parts of the lower McKenzie are open year around.

A No Nonsense Display of

Common Game Fish
In Central & Southeastern Oregon

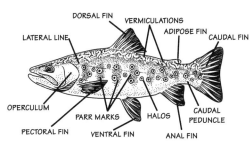

Typical trout, salmon or char.

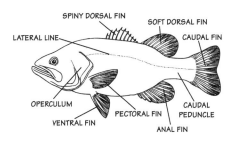

Typical bass, perch, crappie.

BROWN TROUT
Brown colored back with big black spots. A square tail and black and red spots on sides with light blue rings. Hard to catch, easily spooked.

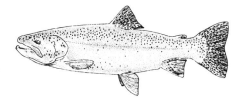

STEELHEAD TROUT
These trout leave rivers for the ocean and return to spawn several times. Similar to rainbows but with fewer spots, bigger and stronger. The tongue tip has teeth, but not the tongue back. Great fighting fish.

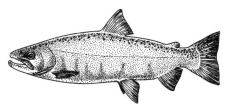

KOKANEE SALMON
Green-blue back with speckles. Sides and belly silver. Fall spawning turns color to dark red, leathery skin with green head. Male snout hooks and back humps, female body shape stays like trout.

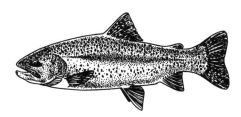

RAINBOW TROUT
The most abundant wild and hatchery fish. An olive-bluish back with small black spots. Sides have light red or pink band. Lake 'bows are often all silver.

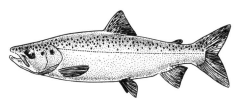

LANDLOCKED ATLANTIC SALMON
Green back, silvery sides, large irregular spots. Deeply forked tail.

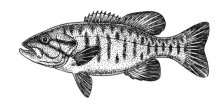

SMALLMOUTH BASS
Dark brown back with vertical bronze stripes on the sides. Spiny dorsal fin (9-10 spines) hasn't a deep notch separating the soft dorsal fin.

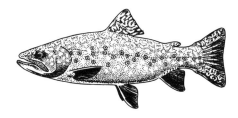

BROOK TROUT
Actually char (Dolly Varden, Bull Trout, Lake Trout, etc.). Black, blue-gray or green back, mottled light colored markings. Sides have red spots with blue rings. Square tail. Lower fins red, striped with black and white. Prefers colder water.

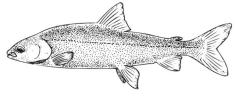

MOUNTAIN WHITEFISH
Light brown to white-ish, split tail. Mouth smaller than trout and doesn't extend back past the eye.

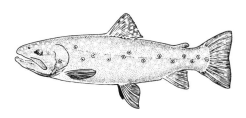

BULL TROUT
In the char family. Back color is light-gray or green. White spots cover back and sides. Indented or split tail.

Illustrations by Pete Chadwell. For fine art and fish renderings write to:
Dynamic Arts 1832 N.E. Providence Dr. • Bend, OR 97701.

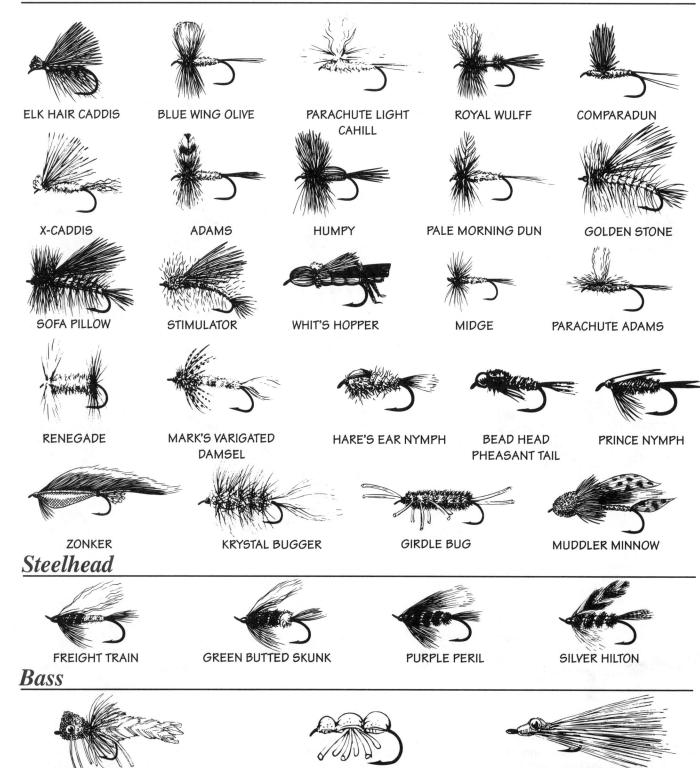

Trout

ELK HAIR CADDIS

BLUE WING OLIVE

PARACHUTE LIGHT CAHILL

ROYAL WULFF

COMPARADUN

X-CADDIS

ADAMS

HUMPY

PALE MORNING DUN

GOLDEN STONE

SOFA PILLOW

STIMULATOR

WHIT'S HOPPER

MIDGE

PARACHUTE ADAMS

RENEGADE

MARK'S VARIGATED DAMSEL

HARE'S EAR NYMPH

BEAD HEAD PHEASANT TAIL

PRINCE NYMPH

ZONKER

KRYSTAL BUGGER

GIRDLE BUG

MUDDLER MINNOW

Steelhead

FREIGHT TRAIN

GREEN BUTTED SKUNK

PURPLE PERIL

SILVER HILTON

Bass

WHITLOCK'S DEER HAIR POPPER

RUBBER LEGS

CLOUSER MINNOW DEEP WATER

Illustrations by Pete Chadwell. For fine art and fish renderings write to: Pete Chadwell •1832 N.E. Providence Dr. • Bend, OR 97701.

Top
Central and
Southeastern Oregon
Fly Fishing Waters

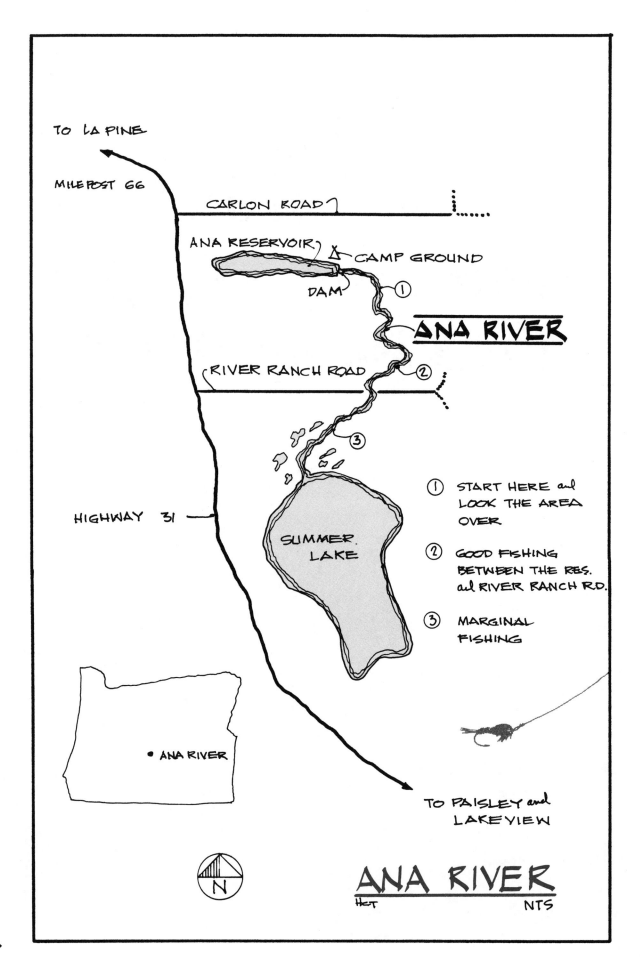

TO LA PINE

MILEPOST 66

CARLON ROAD

ANA RESERVOIR

CAMP GROUND

DAM ①

ANA RIVER

RIVER RANCH ROAD ②

③

① START HERE and LOOK THE AREA OVER

② GOOD FISHING BETWEEN THE RES. and RIVER RANCH RD.

③ MARGINAL FISHING

HIGHWAY 31

SUMMER LAKE

• ANA RIVER

TO PAISLEY and LAKEVIEW

N

ANA RIVER
HcT   NTS

Ana River

*T*he Ana River offers a unique fly fishing experience in an honest-to-God desert river. It flows through a sand and sagebrush open landscape that is genuine Oregon High Desert.

The Ana is only about seven miles long, doesn't get much pressure and holds some nice-sized rainbow trout. It flows from the Ana Reservoir and discharges into Summer Lake. The river's true origins are springs that are now covered by the Ana Reservoir.

You'll work for what you get, and at times it can be frustrating because you can't get a fish to rise. If you like fly fishing challenges, you'll like the Ana's clear water and the need to make good fly presentations.

In a weekends time it is possible to fish the Ana River, Ana Reservoir, Lake of the Dunes and the Chewaucan River. All of these waters are described in this guide. Ana River lies easterly of Highway 31 in the Great Basin near Summer Lake. If you are visiting Central Oregon, the Ana is about a two hour drive from Bend and is a good alternative to some of the areas' more crowded waters.

Type of Fish
Mostly rainbow trout. These fish run from 8" to 16" and are great fighters.

Equipment to Use
Rods: 7 to 9' rods from 2 to 5 weight.
Line: Floating, to match rod weight.
Leaders: 5x and 6x, 9' to 12'.
Reels: Palm drag.
Wading: Neoprene waders with boots. You can fish much of this river without wading, however, I suggest you take the time to walk a quarter of a mile of it so you can determine if you want to wade. A wading staff is a good idea.

Flies to Use
You'll find an abundance of midges, mayflies and terrestrials around the river.
Dry patterns: Adams, Pale Morning Dun, Renegade, Spinner, Callibaetis, Comparadun, Blue Wing Olive, Trico, X Caddis, Henryville, CDC Caddis, and Slow Water Caddis.
Nymphs: Hare's Ear, Chironomid Pupa, Zug Bug, Scud, Brassie, Serendipity, and Pheasant Tail.

When to Fish
Best to fish in May-June and September-October. The Ana River fishes best in the early morning and late evening.

Seasons & Limits
Generally this river is open year around. Because regulations are subject to change, consult the Oregon Department of Fish and Wildlife synopsis or a local fly shop before fishing.

Accommodations & Services
There is a store, restaurant, motel and gas at Summer Lake. There are camping facilities near the dam at Ana Reservoir.

Harry's Opinion
If you happen to hit one of those good days, you'll come back for more of the Ana.

Rating
A soft 4.

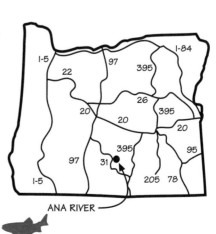

ANA RIVER

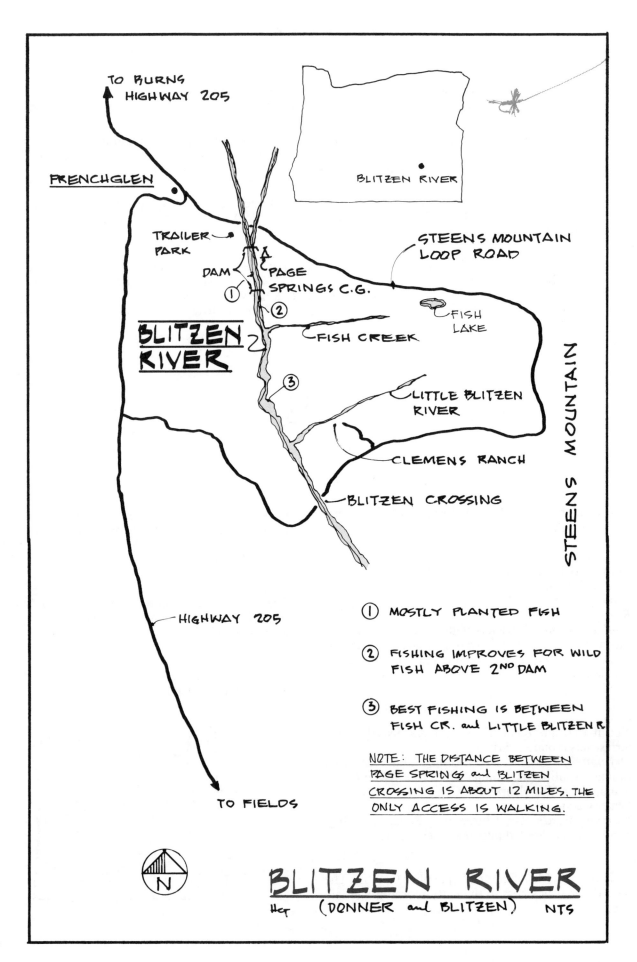

TO BURNS
HIGHWAY 205

FRENCHGLEN

BLITZEN RIVER

TRAILER
PARK

DAM

PAGE
SPRINGS C.G.

①

②

③

FISH CREEK

BLITZEN RIVER

STEENS MOUNTAIN
LOOP ROAD

FISH
LAKE

LITTLE BLITZEN
RIVER

CLEMENS RANCH

BLITZEN CROSSING

STEENS MOUNTAIN

HIGHWAY 205

TO FIELDS

① MOSTLY PLANTED FISH

② FISHING IMPROVES FOR WILD
FISH ABOVE 2ND DAM

③ BEST FISHING IS BETWEEN
FISH CR. and LITTLE BLITZEN R.

NOTE: THE DISTANCE BETWEEN
PAGE SPRINGS and BLITZEN
CROSSING IS ABOUT 12 MILES, THE
ONLY ACCESS IS WALKING.

N

BLITZEN RIVER
Hcf (DONNER and BLITZEN) NTS

Blitzen River

I'm one happy person when I'm in this remote section of Oregon and fishing the Blitzen. If I could design my own trout stream, I'd use the Blitzen above Page Springs as a model. The Blitzen originates in the Steens Mountain, one of the most scenic regions in Oregon.

The Donner and Blitzen, or "Thunder and Lightning" refers to just one river. The two names for one water have to do with a big thunder storm encountered by Army troops who were crossing the river in 1864. The river is commonly referred to as just "The Blitzen". The storms over the Steens Mountain area can get your attention, so bring along rain gear, even in the summer.

This is a wonderful trout stream that requires lots of walking to get to the best fishing. Hardy rainbows are your reward. The river above Page Springs flows through a relatively narrow canyon that's lined with juniper and pine trees. If you like small, remote, desert streams the Blitzen will fulfill one of your fly fishing fantasies.

The Blitzen is located about 65 miles south of Burns, Oregon near the community of Frenchglen. Highway 205 from Burns to Frenchglen is paved. From Frenchglen to the Page Springs campground, about three miles, the road is gravel.

Type of Fish
Rainbow trout, from 8" to 14". However, fish up to 20" are taken on regular basis.

Equipment to Use
Rods: 1 to 5 weight rods, 6 1/2 - 9'.
Line: Floating to match your rod weight.
Leaders: 4x and 5x leaders, 9'.
Reels: Palm or mechanical drag.
Wading: Since you will do a lot of walking, make sure your wading equipment is comfortable and fits properly. Here's what I do when fishing the Blitzen: I take the felt-soled, wading boots that I normally use with my neoprenes, put on neoprene socks and wade in my everyday fishing pants. Yes, I get wet up to my thighs, but on a hot day in the Blitzen Canyon, the cool water is a welcome relief. Lightweight nylon hippers with wading boots are easy to wear when walking.

Flies to Use
Depending on the time of year you fish the Blitzen, you'll find you'll need to adapt your pattern selection to what's happening on the river. There is one fly I've found that fishes well, regardless of the time of year, the Royal Wulff size #14.
Dry patterns: Royal Wulff, Comparadun, Elk Hair Caddis, Adams, Hopper, Renegade and Humpy.
Nymphs & streamers: Woolly Bugger, Prince, Hare's Ear, Muddler, Sculpin, Pheasant Tail and Bead Heads.

When to Fish
Fishing the Blitzen from mid-July through October has been best for me. April and May fishing can be OK but, depending on runoff, the river can be high and out of shape. Fishing in the late afternoon and evening is generally most productive.

Season & Limits
Generally this is an April - October fly fishing stream. Check the Oregon Department of Fish and Wildlife synopsis for exact dates and limits.

Accommodations & Services
At Frenchglen, there is a small hotel with food service, a store, gas, and not much else. At Page Springs, there is a wonderful Bureau of Land Management campground. A private trailer park is located near Page Springs campground which has limited supplies and rents trailers for overnight accommodations.

Harry's Opinion
The Blitzen is a delicate resource that needs our protection. It can stand a reasonable amount of fishing and recreational pressure if we all practice intelligent conservation. I strongly recommend you practice catch and release on this stream.

Rating
Remote, good trout, a strong 6.5.

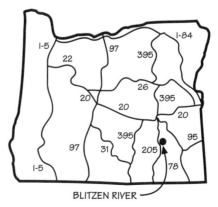

BLITZEN RIVER

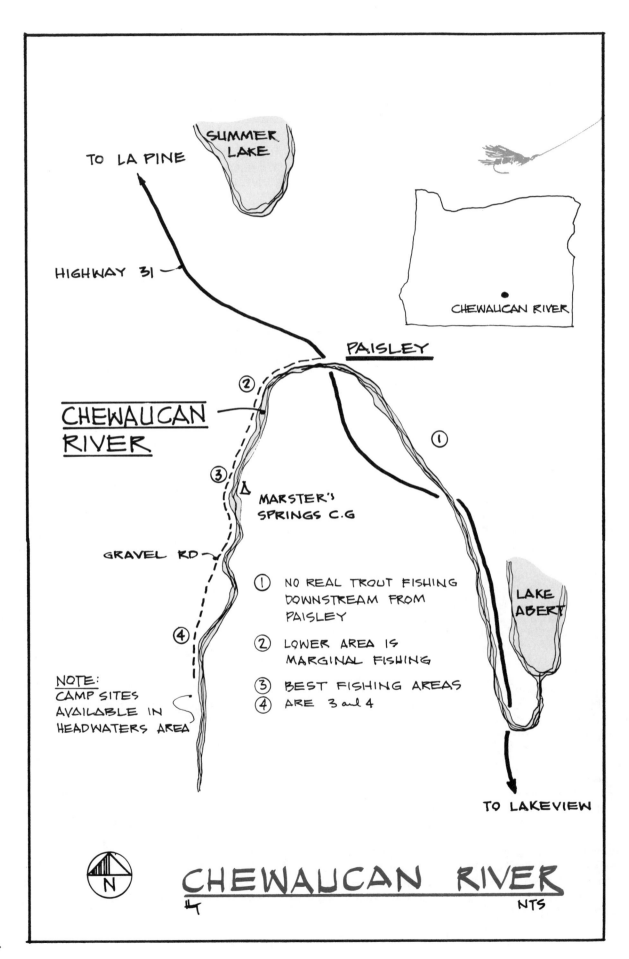

TO LA PINE

SUMMER LAKE

HIGHWAY 31

PAISLEY

CHEWAUCAN RIVER

②

CHEWAUCAN RIVER

③

MARSTER'S SPRINGS C.G

GRAVEL RD

①

LAKE ABERT

④

CHEWAUCAN RIVER

CHEWAUCAN RIVER

① NO REAL TROUT FISHING DOWNSTREAM FROM PAISLEY

② LOWER AREA IS MARGINAL FISHING

③ BEST FISHING AREAS

④ ARE 3 and 4

NOTE:
CAMP SITES AVAILABLE IN HEADWATERS AREA

TO LAKEVIEW

N

CHEWAUCAN RIVER

NTS

Chewaucan River

*T*he Chewaucan is not a big river, but one that is enjoyable to fish with a fly rod. It's a pretty river, off the beaten path, and not very crowded. If you are in the area fishing the Ana or Lake of The Dunes and want a more forested setting or a different place, give the Chewaucan a try.

The Chewaucan flows out of the mountains and heads for the Great Basin, where it dissipates into the Oregon desert. As you go upstream from Paisley you enter the Fremont National Forest. Much of the fishable river lies in this pine studded drainage.

The Chewaucan river is near the small town of Paisley, on Highway 31. You'll need to turn to the south, just west of Paisley, to access the best fishing part of the river. Paisley is a good rest stop when travelling through this rural area. Don't forget mosquito repellent. You'll need it!

Type of Fish
Predominantly planted rainbow trout from 8" to 12", however, there are some nice fish in the 14" to 16" range that are taken on a regular basis.

Equipment to Use
Rods: 3, 4 and 5 weight, 7 - 9'.
Line: Match floating and sink tip to rod weight.
Leaders: 4x and 5x, 9'.
Reels: Palm drag.
Wading: Felt-soled hip boots are OK, but you'll be better off with light waders with felt-soled wading shoes.

Flies to Use
Dry patterns: Pale Morning Dun, Adams, Renegade, Royal Wulff, Mosquito, Comparadun, Elk Hair Caddis, H & L Variant, X Caddis, Humpy, CDC Caddis and Madam X, Blue Winged Olive.
Nymphs: Pheasant Tail, Hare's Ear, Zug Bug, Caddis Pupa, Bead Head Soft Hackle P.T., Beadhead Flashback Hare's Ear and Beadhead Prince.

When to Fish
Regulars on the Chewaucan seem to prefer July through October. Late afternoon and evening are generally the best times to fish.

Season & Limits
The Chewaucan usually opens in late April and closes in late October. These dates can change. Check with a fly shop or consult the Oregon Department Of Fish and Wildlife synopsis for exact dates and limits.

Accommodations & Services
The town of Paisley has a service station, diner and motel. Same services at Summer Lake which also, at this writing, has a B&B. There is camping at selected spots along the river.

Harry's Opinion
I like the Chewaucan. Even though it's not a highly rated stream, I feel it's worth the trip. Exploring new territory is part of the fun of fly fishing.

Rating
The Chewaucan is a 4. If you hit "One of those days," it can be an 8 or 9.

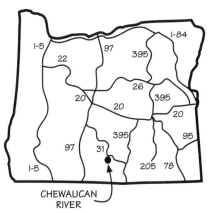

CHEWAUCAN
RIVER

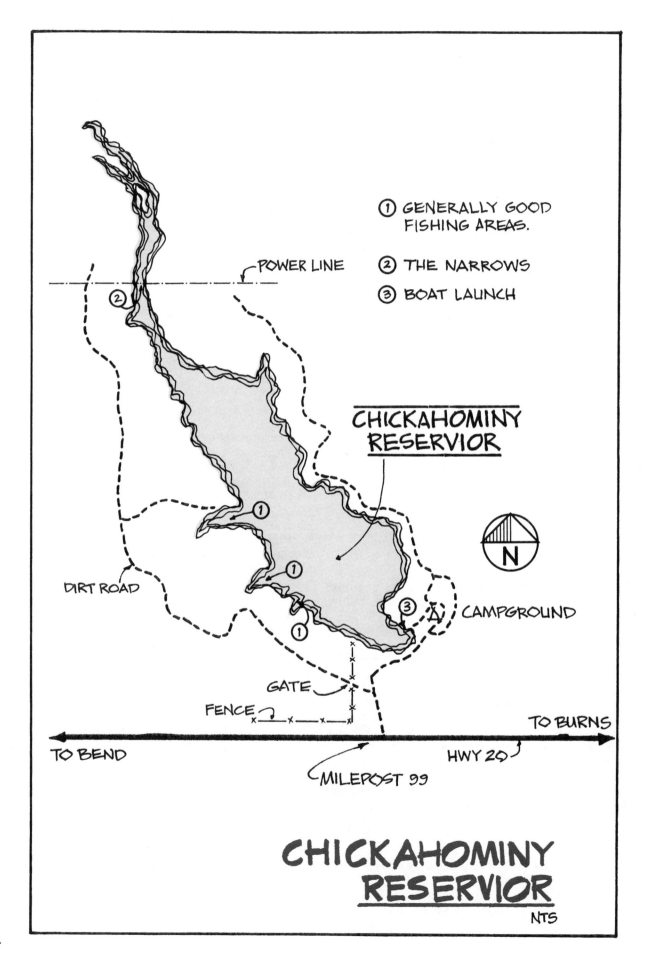

① GENERALLY GOOD
    FISHING AREAS.

② THE NARROWS

③ BOAT LAUNCH

POWER LINE

CHICKAHOMINY
RESERVIOR

N

DIRT ROAD

CAMPGROUND

GATE

FENCE

TO BURNS

TO BEND

HWY 20

MILEPOST 99

CHICKAHOMINY
RESERVIOR

NTS

Chickahominy Reservoir

*C*hickahominy grows big fish and grows them fast. The rainbows, planted here annually, will grow to better than 20 inches. Indications are, they grow up to 2 inches a month during the summer season.

This reservoir is in dry, high desert country, about 100 miles east of Bend. It's a favorite of Bend area anglers and others traveling the east-west route from Idaho, or Burns to Central Oregon. It was developed by the Oregon Department of Fish and Wildlife as an angler's reservoir. It's a good sized body of water covering roughly 500 acres.

Fly fish the reservoir as you would most others. The best results have been with wet patterns or streamers. Fish them near the rocky shore and weed beds. Let the fly sink and strip it in with irregular tugs of 4-6 inches of line. Float tubers should do the same or, let a Prince, Woolly Bugger, Boatman, Leech or Damsel type pattern sink very deep and retrieve slowly. Sink-tip lines help with this technique.

There's a campground at the reservoir, along with a boat launching ramp. Weather in the spring and fall can be unpredictable, so be prepared for wind and cold. The summer months are generally hot, and fly fishing is poor. A word of caution: *don't* drive on the dirt roads around the reservoir after a rain storm.

Type of Fish
Rainbow trout. The fish are stocked annually as fingerlings and grow rapidly.

Equipment to Use
Rods: 5, 6 or 7 weight, 8 1/2 - 9'.
Line: Floating, sink tip or intermediate.
Leaders: 4x - 5x, 7 to 12'.
Reels: Palm or mechanical drag.
Wading: Chest-high neoprenes with felt-soled wading shoes.
Float Tube: A good way to fish the reservoir, remember fins.

Flies to Use
The best results have been with wet patterns: Prince, Hare's Ear, Zug Bug, Damsels, Woolly Bugger and Carey Special.

When to Fish
You'll find the best fly fishing about a week after the ice melts off, which is about March 15th. You'll have good fishing for about a month. Fishing can be slow in the summer, but it picks up again in late-September until the reservoir freezes.

Season & Limits
The reservoir is open year around. Limits can vary so check with a fly shop or consult the Oregon Department Of Fish and Wildlife synopsis for current information.

Accommodations & Services
There's a camp area at the reservoir and nothing else. Bring whatever you need with you because it's a 40 mile drive to Burns, the nearest town. There is a store and service station at Riley, 7 miles away but the hours of operation can be inconsistent

Harry's Opinion
Chickahominy does not get a lot of pressure, and the fishing can be outstanding. Just be prepared for the weather.

Rating
Spring and fall, it's a 7.5. During the summer, it's a 2.

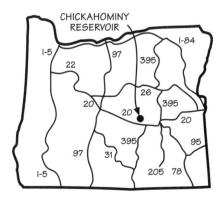

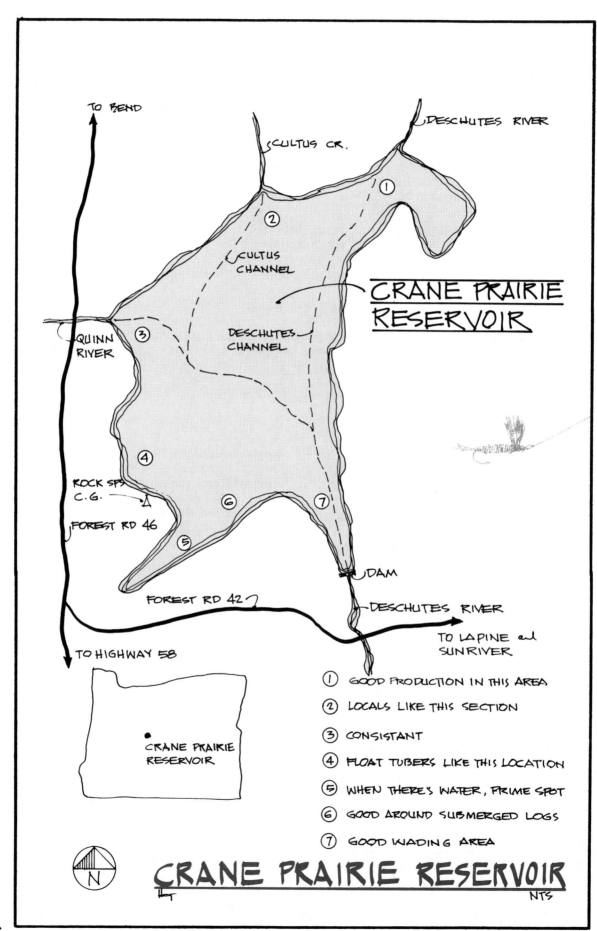

TO BEND

DESCHUTES RIVER

CULTUS CR.

① ②

CULTUS CHANNEL

CRANE PRAIRIE RESERVOIR

DESCHUTES CHANNEL

QUINN RIVER ③

④

ROCK SPS C.G.

⑥ ⑦

FOREST RD 46

⑤

DAM

FOREST RD 42

DESCHUTES RIVER

TO LAPINE and SUNRIVER

TO HIGHWAY 58

CRANE PRAIRIE RESERVOIR

① GOOD PRODUCTION IN THIS AREA

② LOCALS LIKE THIS SECTION

③ CONSISTANT

④ FLOAT TUBERS LIKE THIS LOCATION

⑤ WHEN THERE'S WATER, PRIME SPOT

⑥ GOOD AROUND SUBMERGED LOGS

⑦ GOOD WADING AREA

N

CRANE PRAIRIE RESERVOIR

NTS

Crane Prairie Reservoir

Crane Prairie is one of the finest fly fishing reservoirs in the West. It has more than its share of big trout, scenery and wildlife viewing opportunities. The famed Deschutes river fills this reservoir, and, though the lake is not very deep (11- 20 feet) water levels are fairly consistent. Fish enjoy good cover and plenty of insects.

Most fish the reservoir from a boat or float tube. One can troll large streamers and other wet flies. Nymphing works well early in the season. Fish near Crane's distinctive submerged trees and stick-ups and close to the shoreline when the water is high. In low level conditions look for the two main (submerged) river channels.

Crane Prairie lies west of Bend, Oregon and can be accessed from Century Drive. This is the road past the Mt. Bachelor Ski area and other Cascade lakes. Also look for Forest Highway 46 or Forest Highway 42 from Sunriver.

This is BIG trout water so you'll need equipment that can handle large fish. Bring your larger, heavier weight rods. You'll be glad you did if it is windy and if you get into one of the big fish here.

Type of Fish
You'll find rainbow and brook trout with a fair population of kokanee and illegally introduced bass. The size of trout are amazing: 3 to 5 pound fish are common, and fish in the 10 pound range are recorded annually.

Equipment to Use
Rods: 6 and 7 weight, 9 - 10'.
Line: Matching floating, sink tip or slow sinking lines.
Leaders: 3x - 5x, 9' to 12', fluorocarbon is best.
Reels: Mechanical and palm drag.
Wading: For the most part, fishing from a floating device is most productive. There are a few places where wading can be very rewarding. Try the arm near the dam. Chest-high waders and wading boots are desirable.

Flies to Use
Crane has a real smorgasbord of aquatic food for the trout. Damsel flies, dragon flies, mayflies, scuds and leeches make up a portion of the buffet.

Dry patterns: Parachute Callibaetis, Two Feather May-fly, Captive Dun, Callibaetis Spinner, Timberline Emerger, Comparadun, Adams, Goddard Caddis, Damsel Adult, Slow Water Caddis, Black Elk Hair Caddis, Griffith's Gnat, Palomino, Century Drive Midge, Light Cahill in smaller sizes.
Nymphs: Prince, Scuds, Montana, Pheasant Tail, Snail, Callibaetis, Woolly Bugger, Boatman, Leech, Damsel, Hare's Ear, Dragon, Chironomid, San Juan Worm.

Season & Limits
The season opens in late April and closes the end of October. For exact dates and limit regulations, refer to the ODFW Synopsis.

Accommodations & Services
Crane Prairie is blessed with good camping facilities. There is a store, food service and gas available at the resort at Gails Landing. In the vicinity, there is Twin Lakes Resort and complete services at Sunriver, La Pine and Bend.

Harry's Opinion
If you only have time to fish one place on your trip to Central Oregon and want the opportunity to catch trophy fish, test your skills at Crane Prairie Reservoir.

Rating
An 8.5.

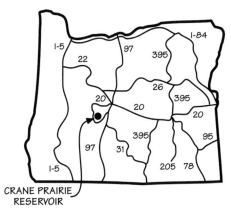

CRANE PRAIRIE RESERVOIR

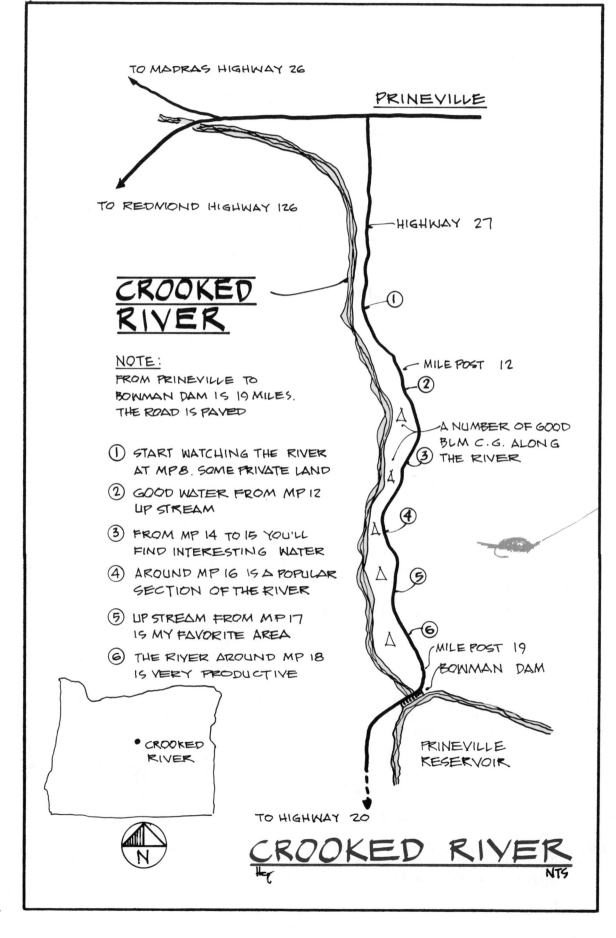

TO MADRAS HIGHWAY 26

PRINEVILLE

TO REDMOND HIGHWAY 126

HIGHWAY 27

CROOKED RIVER

NOTE:
FROM PRINEVILLE TO
BOWMAN DAM IS 19 MILES.
THE ROAD IS PAVED

MILE POST 12

A NUMBER OF GOOD
BLM C.G. ALONG
THE RIVER

① START WATCHING THE RIVER
   AT MP 8. SOME PRIVATE LAND

② GOOD WATER FROM MP 12
   UP STREAM

③ FROM MP 14 TO 15 YOU'LL
   FIND INTERESTING WATER

④ AROUND MP 16 IS A POPULAR
   SECTION OF THE RIVER

⑤ UP STREAM FROM MP 17
   IS MY FAVORITE AREA

⑥ THE RIVER AROUND MP 18
   IS VERY PRODUCTIVE

MILE POST 19
BOWMAN DAM

PRINEVILLE
RESERVOIR

• CROOKED
   RIVER

TO HIGHWAY 20

N

CROOKED RIVER

NTS

Crooked River

*T*his is the river most Central Oregon fly fishers head to when winter weather is bad and fishing is off in other places. The primary fishing section of the Crooked is often under clear and dry midwinter skies and the only game in town. This section lies south of the city of Prineville.

The 19 miles from Prineville to Bowman Dam is reached off paved State Highway 27 which parallels the river. The Crooked River below Bowman Dam is a wonderful tailrace stream. That is, it's wonderful when the Bureau of Reclamation releases an adequate amount of water (minimum of 75 cfs) to truly sustain this quality fishery. From mile post 12 to 19, which is really the prime area, you'll find interesting water with plenty of riffles and pools.

The area's geographical features are impressive. High basalt walls and juniper, pine and sage-covered flats create an environment right out of a wild west movie set. Most of the time the water is off color, but don't let that bother you, it doesn't seem to bother the fish. The basic food of the fish here is a fresh water shrimp. They're in the river by the zillions.

The Crooked River is primarily a nymphing stream. Dry fly activity can be good, but you have to be there when the hatch is on. Day in and day out, most fish are taken subsurface. In my opinion the Crooked fishes well all day long, with the best time in the late afternoon and evening.

Type of Fish
Rainbows, cutthroats and a rainbow-cutthroat cross. Most fish will run from 8" to 12", but you'll get a fair number in the 13" to 18" range. We've seen pictures of 6 plus pound fish, but I haven't hooked one.

Equipment to Use
Rods: 1 to 5 weight.
Line: Match to rod weight. A great nymphing stream, but floating lines with weighted nymphs produce.
Leaders: 5x and 6x, 9'.
Reels: Palm drag.
Wading: The Crooked is not necessarily difficult to wade if you use good judgment, but it's tricky. There are lots of boulders that can cause embarrassing problems, not life threatening, but obstacles that can make you look like an unskilled gymnast. I suggest you have felt-soled, wading boots, a wading staff and at least waist-high neoprenes.

Flies to Use.
Dry patterns: Adams, Comparadun, Elk Hair Caddis, Renegade, Griffith's Gnat, Midge Pupa, Palomino, BWO, Knock Down Dun, Hi-Viz Parachute.
Nymphs: Scuds, Beadhead Prince, Hare's Ear, Scuds and Brassie Scuds, Pheasant Tail, Soft Hackles, Woolly Bugger Serendipities Beadhead Mayfly. Use a strike indicator for nymphs.

When to Fish
The Crooked is open year-round, so you should fish it whenever you've got the time. However, there are times in the winter months when the Crooked is frozen over, so check first.

Season & Limits
The Crooked is open year round, but subject to change. There are restrictions on fish limits and fishing methods. Refer to the Oregon Department of Fish and Wildlife synopsis for current information.

Accommodations & Services
There are fine camping areas, provided by the BLM, all along the river. Lodging can be found 25 miles away in Prineville. There's a full range of services available including restaurants, groceries, lodging, gas and automotive services.

Harry's Opinion
I like the Crooked from mile post 12 to 18. There are plenty of fish and it's a good stream for all skill levels.

Rating
A 6.5.

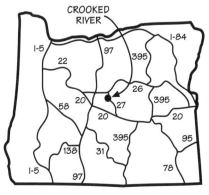

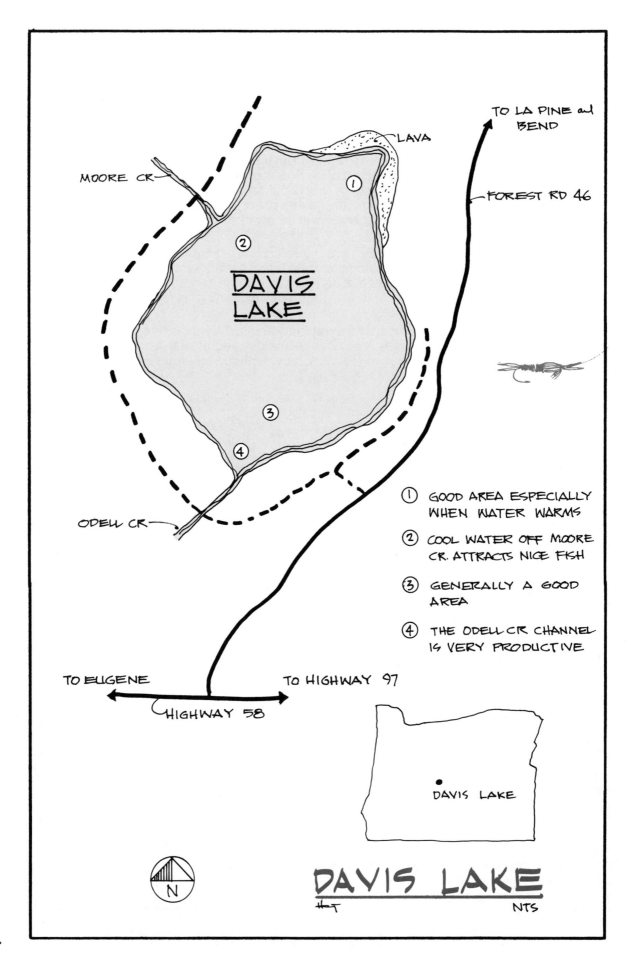

MOORE CR

LAVA

TO LA PINE and
BEND

FOREST RD 46

①

②

DAVIS
LAKE

③

④

ODELL CR

① GOOD AREA ESPECIALLY
   WHEN WATER WARMS

② COOL WATER OFF MOORE
   CR. ATTRACTS NICE FISH

③ GENERALLY A GOOD
   AREA

④ THE ODELL CR CHANNEL
   IS VERY PRODUCTIVE

TO EUGENE

TO HIGHWAY 97

HIGHWAY 58

DAVIS LAKE

DAVIS LAKE

N

NTS

Davis Lake

W hen Davis is right, it's one fine and challenging fishery. It's only about 25 feet deep and is thick with bugs. Catch and release fishing has taught the large trout to remain even more sceptical than usual.

Davis Lake is located in both Deschutes and Klamath Counties. It's about 9 miles past Crane Prairie and Wickiup Reservoirs and Twin Lakes. If any of these other waters are off, go a little father south to Davis. Use Forest Route 46, west of La Pine, Oregon.

Davis has been managed for fly angling only and has generally lived up to it's responsibility of providing big trout. During the Central Oregon drought period of the late 80's, however, the lake suffered from low water conditions and relatively poor fishing was the norm. Disease also reduced the number and hardiness of Davis trout. Water levels, however, have improved and the lake is returning to its glory days.

As of this writing, fishing while using a motor is prohibited. You can use a motor to get to the fishing spot, however, which is a benefit on a lake some 3 miles across. Use a float tube just about anywhere on the lake during cool water months. During summer, most of the fish head toward the inlets and the lava dam area. Nymphing is generally the best technique on Davis, but dries can be productive.

Type of Fish
Primarily rainbow trout; however, other species have been introduced by ODFW. When Davis is at its best, 2 to 5 pound trout are common.

Equipment to Use
Rods: 5, 6 and 7 weight, 8 1/2 - 9 1/2'.
Line: Floating and sink tip to match rod weight.
Leaders: 4x and 5x, 9'.
Reels: Mechanical and palm drag.
Wading: You can wade some portions of the lake. Best you have chest-high neoprenes with wading boots. Davis is a good float-tubing lake, especially around the O'Dell Creek channel. Boats (type and design of your choice) are in order. There are launching sites at all the camp grounds.

Flies to Use
Davis is rich with aquatic life. There are midge, mayfly and mosquito hatches.
Dry patterns: Parachute Callibaetis, Two Feather Mayfly, Captive Dun, Callibaetis Spinner, Timberline Emerger, Comparadun, Adams, Goddard Caddis, Damsel Adult, Slow Water Caddis, Black Elk Hair Caddis, Griffith's Gnat, Palomino, Century Drive Midge, Light Cahill in smaller sizes.
Nymphs: Prince, Scuds, Montana, Pheasant Tail, Snails, Callibaetis Nymph, Woolly Bugger, Boatman, Leech, Damsel, Hare's Ear Chironomid, San Juan Worm, Dragon Fly.

When to Fish
Good fishing, when the water is right, is available throughout the season. I feel the best time is late-May or June and again in late-September and October. My experience is that Davis fishes well all day long.

Season & Limits
Open all year but, before fishing, review the ODFW synopsis for exact dates and limit regulations.

Accommodations & Services
There are excellent campgrounds at Davis, but for most other services you'll have to drive to La Pine, Sunriver or Bend. There are resorts at South Twin Lake and Crane Prairie that have restaurants, groceries and gas.

Harry's Opinion
Davis has an abundance of food that grows big fish. Along with the recent introduction of a different strain of rainbow trout, Davis is one of the prime fly fishing lakes in Oregon.

Rating
Davis is a solid 7.

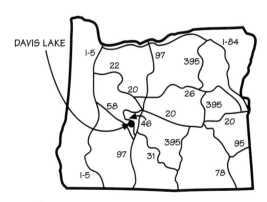

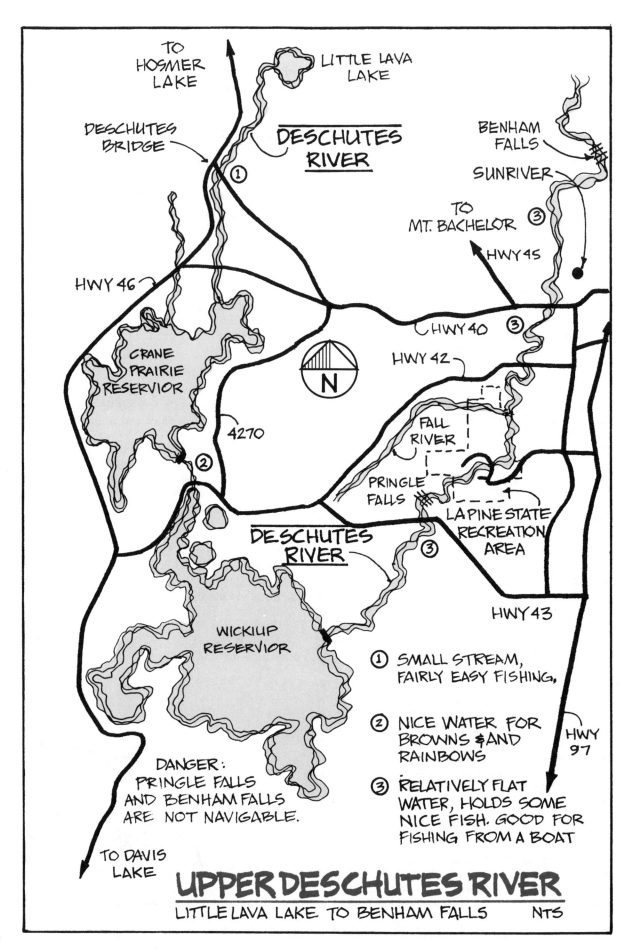

TO
HOSMER
LAKE

LITTLE LAVA
LAKE

DESCHUTES
BRIDGE

DESCHUTES
RIVER

①

BENHAM
FALLS

SUNRIVER

TO
MT. BACHELOR

③

③

HWY 45

HWY 46

HWY 40

HWY 42

CRANE
PRAIRIE
RESERVIOR

N

4270

FALL
RIVER

②

PRINGLE
FALLS

③

LA PINE STATE
RECREATION
AREA

DESCHUTES
RIVER

③

HWY 43

WICKIUP
RESERVIOR

① SMALL STREAM,
FAIRLY EASY FISHING.

② NICE WATER FOR
BROWNS & AND
RAINBOWS

HWY
97

DANGER:
PRINGLE FALLS
AND BENHAM FALLS
ARE NOT NAVIGABLE.

③ RELATIVELY FLAT
WATER, HOLDS SOME
NICE FISH. GOOD FOR
FISHING FROM A BOAT

TO DAVIS
LAKE

UPPER DESCHUTES RIVER
LITTLE LAVA LAKE TO BENHAM FALLS   NTS

Deschutes River

*I*f I only had one river to fish, the Deschutes would be it. It has it all: beauty, variety of fish, challenging water and a true test of fly fishing skills. Yet, it's possible to take a real neophyte to the river and, with some assistance, get him or her into fish.

For these, and other reasons, the Deschutes is probably the finest overall fly fishing river in Western America. Its complement of big Redside trout, salmon, steelhead and whitefish, offers a wide range of high quality fly fishing. The river lies east of the Cascade Mountains and runs, mostly north, from Little Lava Lake into the Columbia River east of the town of The Dalles.

Fishing access is good for a river of this size. Along the banks there are paved roads, gravel roads, railroad tracks, mountain bike trails and hiking paths. Where there is not access, float trips, guided and otherwise, are popular ways to get to prime locations. As the river settings change from mature pine forests to sheer basalt canyons with desert vegetation, a scenic trip is always a pleasant bi-product of an outing on the Deschutes. Drift boats are used for transportation, but you have to get out of the boat to fish most of the Deschutes.

This is a match-the-hatch river where you'll find a full range of midges, mayflies, caddis, stones and terrestrials. From late-April to October use various nymphs for trout. Dry fly action picks up mid-May and runs through October. Late May through mid-June catch the salmon fly frenzy, then an exceptional caddis and mayfly hatch lasting through September. In October small mayflies, caddis and midges often bring feeding trout to the surface. When in doubt, consult a local fly shop for current activity.

The Deschutes summer-run steelhead is a world-class fish! The popularity of fly fishing for them has increased greatly in the last few years. Because fly angling for these amazing fish is somewhat different than trout angling, a special page and map of the lower river and steelhead section of the Deschutes is presented after this overview section.

Note that three maps follow and divide the river into broad sections: upper, middle and lower. In general, the upper section of the Deschutes runs amid Ponderosa forests and meanders through the resort of Sunriver. The middle section flows through the town of Bend, through the Crooked River Ranch subdivision and into and out of Lake Billy Chinook, Lake Simtustus and to Sherars Falls.

The lower river begins at Sherars Falls where the river makes a dramatic, unnavigable, 25 foot drop and eventually joins the mighty Columbia River. The steelhead map covers fishing this lower portion of the river.

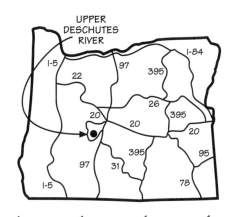

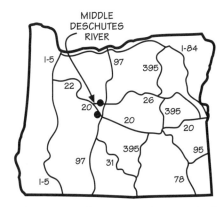

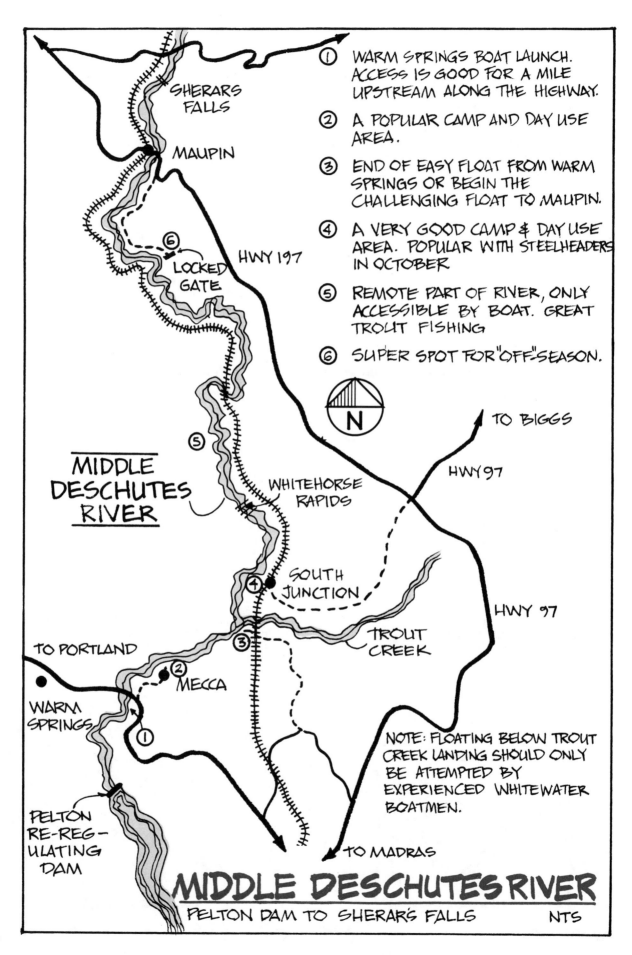

① WARM SPRINGS BOAT LAUNCH. ACCESS IS GOOD FOR A MILE UPSTREAM ALONG THE HIGHWAY.

② A POPULAR CAMP AND DAY USE AREA.

③ END OF EASY FLOAT FROM WARM SPRINGS OR BEGIN THE CHALLENGING FLOAT TO MAUPIN.

④ A VERY GOOD CAMP & DAY USE AREA. POPULAR WITH STEELHEADERS IN OCTOBER

⑤ REMOTE PART OF RIVER, ONLY ACCESSIBLE BY BOAT. GREAT TROUT FISHING

⑥ SUPER SPOT FOR "OFF" SEASON.

N

TO BIGGS
HWY 97

HWY 97

SHERARS FALLS

MAUPIN

HWY 197

LOCKED GATE

⑥

⑤

MIDDLE DESCHUTES RIVER

WHITEHORSE RAPIDS

SOUTH JUNCTION

④

③

TROUT CREEK

TO PORTLAND

② MECCA

①

WARM SPRINGS

NOTE: FLOATING BELOW TROUT CREEK LANDING SHOULD ONLY BE ATTEMPTED BY EXPERIENCED WHITEWATER BOATMEN.

PELTON RE-REG-ULATING DAM

TO MADRAS

MIDDLE DESCHUTES RIVER
PELTON DAM TO SHERAR'S FALLS   NTS

Deschutes River

continued

Type of Fish
Predominantly rainbow trout. Steelhead during their spawning runs. Some bull trout and browns. Whitefish can supply some exciting fishing.

Equipment to Use
From Crane Prairie Reservoir, the Deschutes is a relatively small meandering stream. From Wickiup Reservoir it becomes a full-flowing "Big River". The majority of the quality fishing is on this part. Equipment listed below is for trout.

Rods: 3 to 6 weight, 8 - 10'.
Line: Floating and sink tip to match rod weight.
Leaders: 5x - 6x, 12', for dries. 4x - 5x 9' for nymphs, with strike indicator.
Reels: Disc drag is best.
Wading: Always a challenge here. Wear chest-high waders with felt-soled wading shoes or stream cleats and take a wading staff. Use your best wading sense in the Deschutes!

Flies to Use
Dry patterns: Adams, Elk Hair Caddis, Blue Wing Olive, Slow Water Caddis, Henryville, CDC Caddis, Knock Down Dun, Clark's Stone, March Brown, Griffith's Gnat, X Caddis, Comparadun, Pale Morning Dun, Renegade, Salmon Flies and October Caddis.

Nymphs: Girdle Bug, Hare's Ear, Kaufmann's Stone, Sparkle Pupa, Feather Duster, Bead Head Pheasant Tail, Prince, Brassie, October Caddis Pupa, Yellow Soft Hackle, Bead Head Serendipity.
Note: In late winter take a #14, #16 and #18 Black Stone. You can experience some exceptional brown trout fishing near Lower Bridge.

When to Fish
Trout fish whenever you can. Evening fishing, in the summer, is far and away the best time. Consider the hatches mentioned above. For steelhead, the best fishing generally starts at the Columbia River (the mouth) about mid-July. Most fish are taken from the mouth to Sherars Falls. September -December fish for steelhead above Sherars Falls to Pelton Dam.

Season & Limits
Seasons and limits vary and are subject to frequent changes. Consult the ODFW synopsis or a local fly shop before fishing. Generally, trout and steelhead fish year 'round on the mid to lower sections. Fish for trout

Accommodations & Services
Upper river: Lodging and food at South Twin Lake, Sunriver and La Pine. The later two have gasoline.

Mid-river: Resorts, motels and all supplies from Bend to Sisters, to Redmond.

Lower river: Store and gas in Madras. Full services at Kahneeta Resort. You can fish a section of the Warm Springs River, adjacent to the resort, with the proper tribal permit. Also, full services in Maupin. The 25 miles from Macks Canyon to the mouth is only accessed by foot or boat except a *very* primitive road at Kloan. Take everything you need into this section because there isn't a corner 7-11. Near the mouth of the Deschutes, motels, restaurant, groceries and gas at Biggs Junction.

Harry & Jeff's Opinion
We've fly fished South America, Alaska and all over the west and the Deschutes is as good as it gets. Spectacular scenery, a good clean river, wild trout and steelhead. This is a "10" in Oregon and the Western United States.

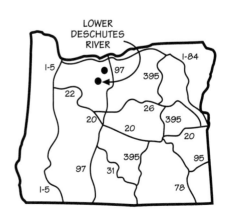

LOWER DESCHUTES RIVER

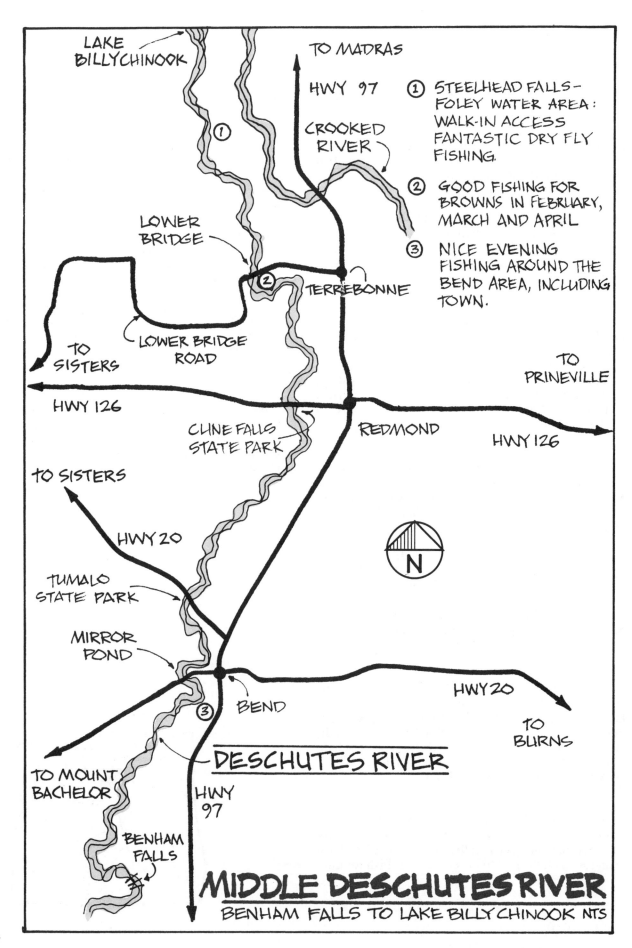

LAKE BILLYCHINOOK

TO MADRAS

HWY 97

CROOKED RIVER

① STEELHEAD FALLS – FOLEY WATER AREA: WALK-IN ACCESS FANTASTIC DRY FLY FISHING.

② GOOD FISHING FOR BROWNS IN FEBRUARY, MARCH AND APRIL

③ NICE EVENING FISHING AROUND THE BEND AREA, INCLUDING TOWN.

LOWER BRIDGE

TERREBONNE

TO SISTERS

LOWER BRIDGE ROAD

TO PRINEVILLE

HWY 126

CLINE FALLS STATE PARK

REDMOND

HWY 126

TO SISTERS

HWY 20

N

TUMALO STATE PARK

MIRROR POND

BEND

HWY 20

TO BURNS

DESCHUTES RIVER

TO MOUNT BACHELOR

HWY 97

BENHAM FALLS

MIDDLE DESCHUTES RIVER
BENHAM FALLS TO LAKE BILLY CHINOOK NTS

Jeff Perin with a classic Deschutes River steelhead. A beautiful result of hours spent casting on one of the most versatile fly fishing rivers in the western United States.

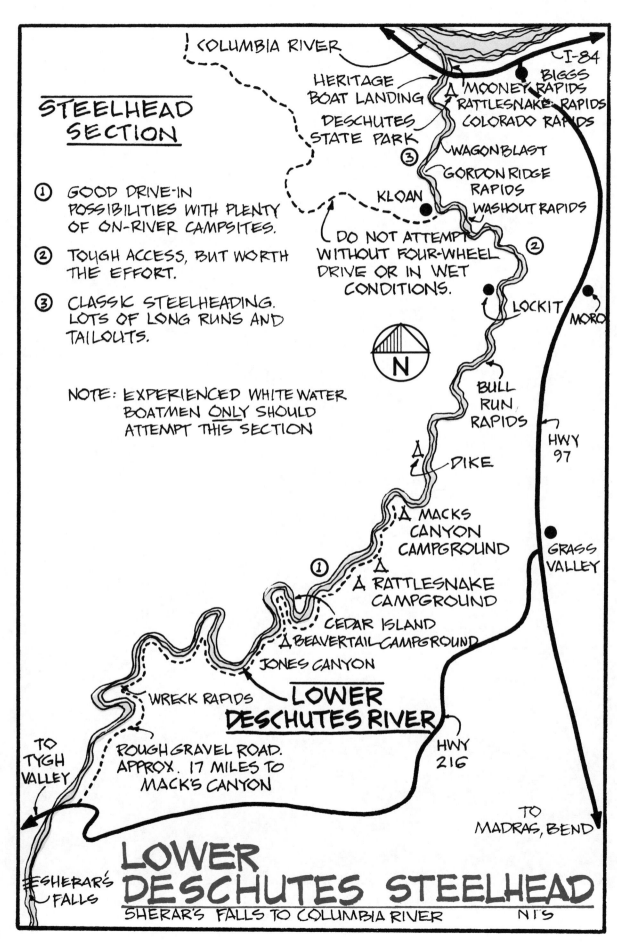

COLUMBIA RIVER

I-84

HERITAGE
BOAT LANDING

MOONEY RAPIDS
RATTLESNAKE RAPIDS
COLORADO RAPIDS

BIGGS

DESCHUTES
STATE PARK

WAGON BLAST

GORDON RIDGE
RAPIDS

③

KLOAN

WASHOUT RAPIDS

STEELHEAD SECTION

① GOOD DRIVE-IN POSSIBILITIES WITH PLENTY OF ON-RIVER CAMPSITES.

② TOUGH ACCESS, BUT WORTH THE EFFORT.

③ CLASSIC STEELHEADING. LOTS OF LONG RUNS AND TAILOUTS.

NOTE: EXPERIENCED WHITE WATER BOATMEN ONLY SHOULD ATTEMPT THIS SECTION

DO NOT ATTEMPT WITHOUT FOUR-WHEEL DRIVE OR IN WET CONDITIONS.

②

LOCKIT

MORO

N

BULL RUN RAPIDS

HWY 97

DIKE

MACKS CANYON CAMPGROUND

① RATTLESNAKE CAMPGROUND

GRASS VALLEY

CEDAR ISLAND
BEAVERTAIL CAMPGROUND

JONES CANYON

LOWER DESCHUTES RIVER

WRECK RAPIDS

HWY 216

TO TYGH VALLEY

ROUGH GRAVEL ROAD. APPROX. 17 MILES TO MACK'S CANYON

TO MADRAS, BEND

LOWER DESCHUTES STEELHEAD

SHERAR'S FALLS TO COLUMBIA RIVER

NTS

SHERAR'S FALLS

Deschutes Steelhead

Steelhead, coming from the ocean and up the mighty Columbia river, start arriving in the Deschutes mid-July. Many local newspapers publish fish count information or call the Oregon Department of Fish and Wildlife (503) 872-5263. Check these counts first. When they reach 1,000 Steelhead a day over Bonneville Dam (or more) it's time. By the way, many of these steelhead are Idaho hatchery fish that detour into the Deschutes every season. It's believed they stray from the warm waters in the Columbia River to the cooler waters in the Deschutes. Now *that's* a wrong turn on a long trip.

From Central Oregon take Highway 97 north to Biggs Junction. Highway 197 accesses the town of Maupin. Highway 216, out of Grass Valley, goes to the Sherars Falls area. From Sherars Falls upstream to Pelton Dam, steelheading is best in the fall. The 44 river miles from Sherars Falls to "the mouth" (where the Deschutes meets the Columbia) is best fly fished late-July through October.

For direct vehicle access use the road from Sherars Falls to Macks Canyon. This 17 miles of gravel follows plenty of water, has many turnouts and is a good bet for a day trip. Better yet, pitch a tent at one of the many BLM sites. Remember your alarm clock and rise early so you're assured of a portion of river before sunup. Steelheading at dawn can be key, though anytime the direct sun is off the water is a prime time to fish for steelhead with a fly.

The Downstream Swing technique works best. Steelhead come up to flies just below or on the surface, so use a floating line. When the water temperature and or level changes, however, Steelhead tend to hunker down. A sink-tip or weighted fly may work best. Steelhead often hold in different water than trout. Fish tailouts or runs that have structure such a as boulders or ledges.

Floating from Buckhollow takes in a beautiful canyon and is a good 1 to 6 day float trip. If boating, be sure you have the experience to run nasty class III and IV whitewater. The *Handbook to the Deschutes River Canyon* is invaluable!

From the Columbia, at Deschutes State Park and Heritage Landing, many fly fishers hike up either side of the river. Riding a mountain bike up the east side trail is also popular. A less arduous trip is via jet boat up through the powerful whitewater. Either way you are entering a prime summer steelhead area.

Type of Fish
Predominantly hatchery-reared steelhead, which have one or more fins clipped for identification. Current regulations allow you to keep hatchery fish only. Let the wild ones go.

Equipment
Rods: 6 to 8 wt., 9 - 10'. Spey, 6 to 9 wt., 11 1/2 - 15'.
Reels: Disc drag, 100 - 200 yards of backing.
Lines: Steelhead taper or weight forward floating, 10' - 13' type III sink-tip, 200 grain sink-tip.
Wading: Chest-high neoprene waders, felt-soled boots and cleats for slippery rocks and swift currents. Regulars use a wading staff or personal flotation device.

Flies to Use
Sparsely tied "low water" patterns are best in purple, black and orange. Purple Peril, Freight Train, Green Butt Skunk, Skunk, Red Wing Blackbird, Mack's Canyon. Weighted flies: Purple Flash, Articulated Leech, Lead Eye Egg Sucking-Woolly Bugger, Girdle Bug, Beadhead Prince.

When to Fish
Usually late July - October is best up to Macks Canyon. August - November is great, Macks Canyon to Sherars Falls. Late September - October, Sherars Falls to Warm Springs is best.

Accommodations & Services
Motels and all services in Biggs Junction and The Dalles, if fishing up from "the mouth". Jacks Fine Foods is a popular dining spot in Biggs. There are more restaurants in The Dalles. If fishing above Macks Canyon, food, service, and motels are found in Grass Valley, Maupin, Madras, Bend, Redmond and Sisters. Camp sites all along the river and at the mouth.

Jeff's Opinion
Since 1991, when Harry Teel introduced me to this fishery, it's become one of my favorites. My wife and I consider these our favorite gamefish and come July we can't wait to go to the lower Deschutes. If you can wade, cast 50', and mend line, you can probably catch a Steelhead here.

Rating
Depending on the run of Steelhead. At least a 6. In a good year, 9 to 10.

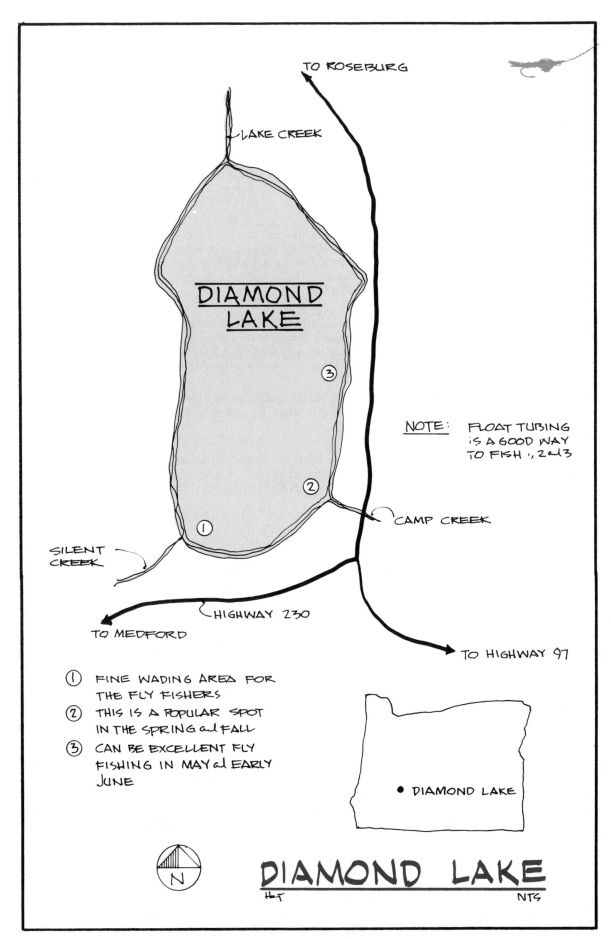

TO ROSEBURG

LAKE CREEK

DIAMOND
LAKE

③

NOTE: FLOAT TUBING
IS A GOOD WAY
TO FISH 1, 2 and 3

②

CAMP CREEK

①

SILENT
CREEK

HIGHWAY 230

TO MEDFORD

TO HIGHWAY 97

① FINE WADING AREA FOR
THE FLY FISHERS

② THIS IS A POPULAR SPOT
IN THE SPRING and FALL

③ CAN BE EXCELLENT FLY
FISHING IN MAY and EARLY
JUNE

● DIAMOND LAKE

N

DIAMOND LAKE

HcT   NTS

Diamond Lake

*T*his may be the most productive lake in the state for trout food and quick growing rainbows. Fish over 5 lbs. are taken each year. People tend to think of Diamond as a trolling and bait fishing lake but you can also have great fly fishing action. This, however, may be changing.

Oregon Department of Fish and Wildlife plans to draw down the lake in the summer of 1999. Unwanted fish will be poisoned. Refilling and restocking will commence in the spring with a hoped for angling season in the summer of 2,000. Large, healthier Williamson Rainbow trout will be reintroduced which should provide thousands of 18" - 20" brutes.

This plan might be underway by the time you read this. Therefore fly fishing Diamond Lake may be either "on hold", poor, recovering or back to pre-draw down glory.

If you decide to, or can fly fish Diamond, consider float tubing in 10 - 20 feet of water and along drop-offs along the west and east shores. Trolling and sink-and-retrieve nymphs and streamers is effective. Use lots of line. Always look out for passing boats which should only be going 10 M.P.H. or less during fishing season. This said, don't forget that wading can be very productive here too, just ask Cal Jordan.

Diamond, at 5,100' elevation, offers a wonderful mountain setting with nearby views of Mt. Bailey and Mt. Thielsen. The heavily forested area has plenty of campgrounds and visitor facilities and is a good place for family camping, fishing and hiking. The short drive to Crater Lake National Park is a "must see" while in Oregon.

Diamond Lake is in Douglas County, well marked and accessed from Highway 138. It's most easily accessed from the east from Highway 97 and Highway 138. From the south and west use Highways 230 and 138.

Type of Fish
Rainbow trout, 10" to 24", averaging 1 lb. plus.

Equipment to Use
Rods: 6 or 7 weight, 9' - 9 1/2'.
Line: Floating line to match rod size.
Leaders: 4x or 5x, 9'.
Reels: Mechanical and palm drag.
Wading: Chest-high waders and boots for float-tubing and wading.

Flies to Use
Midges and mayflies hatch in the spring.
Dry patterns: Midge, Comparadun, Adams, Blue Dun.
Nymphs: Leech, Damsel, Hare's Ear and Chironomids.

When to Fish
Best when the ice thaws in late-April and fish start their spring spawning. Fishing can remain good through May and sometimes early June. It picks up again Sept. - Oct. The lake fishes well nearly all day long.

Season & Limits
Open late-April through the end of October. A 10 fish per day limit has been in effect, but check exact dates and limits in the current ODFW synopsis.

Accommodations & Services
Good campgrounds along the lake. Cabins, food, stores and gas at Diamond Lake Lodge. Several boat ramps.

Harry's Opinion
This *can* be one of the finest lake fisheries in the west with an opportunity to catch plenty of quality trout.

Rating
Diamond Lake, for all types of fishing is a 9. For fly fishing, it's a 7.5.

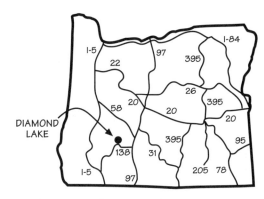

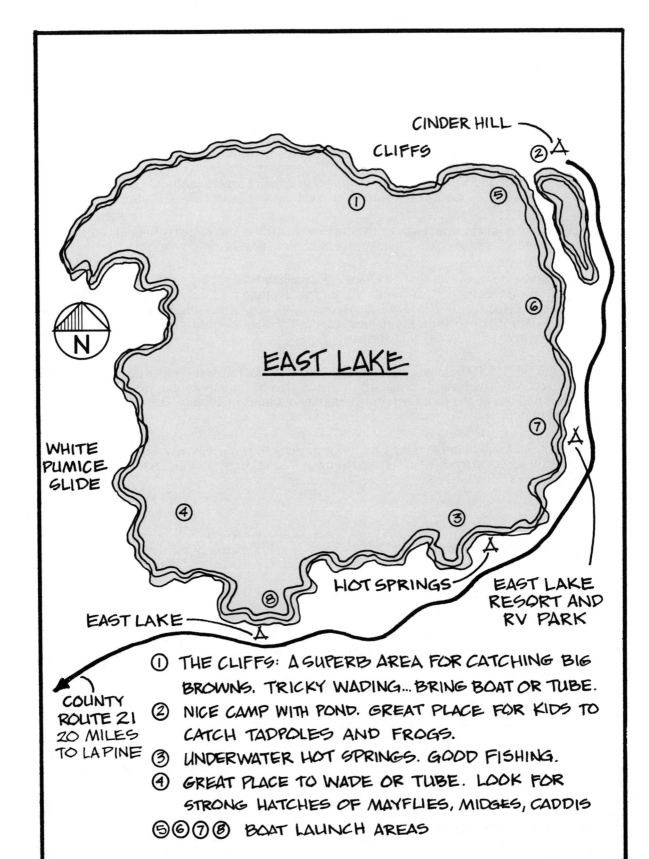

CINDER HILL

CLIFFS

② ⛺

⑤

EAST LAKE

WHITE
PUMICE
SLIDE

N

⑥

⑦ ⛺

④

③

⑧

HOT SPRINGS

EAST LAKE
RESORT AND
RV PARK

EAST LAKE ⛺

COUNTY
ROUTE 21
20 MILES
TO LA PINE

① THE CLIFFS: A SUPERB AREA FOR CATCHING BIG
   BROWNS. TRICKY WADING... BRING BOAT OR TUBE.
② NICE CAMP WITH POND. GREAT PLACE FOR KIDS TO
   CATCH TADPOLES AND FROGS.
③ UNDERWATER HOT SPRINGS. GOOD FISHING.
④ GREAT PLACE TO WADE OR TUBE. LOOK FOR
   STRONG HATCHES OF MAYFLIES, MIDGES, CADDIS
⑤⑥⑦⑧ BOAT LAUNCH AREAS

EAST LAKE
NTS

East Lake

*F*ly fishing possibilities are almost limitless here. This combines with the short drive from Central Oregon's major cities to make East Lake a favorite stillwater.

A roundabout reason for catch and release angling has helped this fishery. A few years back, higher than average levels of mercury were found in East Lake fish. The Health Department recommended not eating them. Almost overnight, East Lake transformed into a great catch and release lake and sizes and numbers of fish improved dramatically.

East Lake is about 1,000 acres and over 170 feet deep in the middle. Water stays cool at this elevation, even in summer. Unlike it's nearby cousin, Paulina Lake, East has vast, weedy and shallow shoreline areas. Scuds, leeches, chironomids, mayflies, caddis and damsels grow in these warmer areas.

Casting for an assortment of feisty fish is exciting. In October, fish streamers for big fish. Wading, boating and float-tubing are all effective methods. Unless you have a motorboat, fish areas close to one of the boat launches or campgrounds.

East Lake has some very good campgrounds. For families with kids, try Cinderhill, where there's a small pond loaded with tadpoles and frogs. East Lake can have a bear or two wandering around. They don't usually bother, but use common sense and don't leave food out overnight. If you have time, take the drive up to Paulina Peak. What a view!

East Lake is easy to get to. From Bend, go south 22 miles on Highway 97, then 20 miles east, up road 21. East Lake is at 6,380 feet in elevation, so snow is possible even in the summer.

Type of Fish
Rainbow, brown, Atlantic Salmon, a few brook trout.

Known Hatches
Callibaetis, chironomid, long-horned caddis, damsel, scuds, crayfish, forage fish and leeches.

Equipment to Use
Rods: 3 - 6 weight, 8 1/2' to 10'.
Line: Floating, intermediate, type II - IV for the deep.
Leaders: 9' to 15', 3x to 6x. 7 1/2' for sinking lines.
Reels: Click or disc drag.
Wading: Neoprene waders and felt-soled boots. Use cleats in the cliff area. Best to use a boat or float tube.

Flies to Use
Dries: Parachute Adams, Callibaetis Spinner, Comparadun, Timberline Emerger, Suspender Midge, Para-Midge, Griffith's Gnat, Black Elk Hair Caddis, X Caddis, Adult Damsel, Ant, Beetle and Float-N-Fool.
Nymphs: Beadhead Leech, Woolly Bugger, Carey Special, Scud, Pheasant Tail, Damsel, Gold Ribbed Hare's Ear, Soft Hackle Hare's Ear, Beadhead Prince.
Streamers: Zonker, Marabou Muddler, Sculpin-Bugger, Crayfish and Bunny Matuka.

When to Fish
Mid to late June through October 1, hatches are prime. Fishing is usually best late mornings and evening.

Seasons & Regulations
Open last Saturday in April to October 31. Ice can be locked in until June. Check at a fly shop for early season fishing. Most fishing techniques are permitted. There's a limit of fish that can be taken.

Accommodations & Services
Good campsites. East Lake Resort has cabins and restaurant (541-536-2230). All services available in La Pine, Sunriver and Bend.

Jeff's Opinion
The 90's helped East Lake and it is now one of the best fly fishing lakes in Central Oregon. Continue to practice catch & release and East will continue to be hot.

Rating
Definitely an 8.

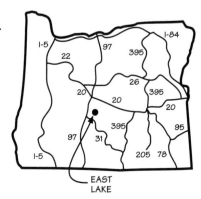

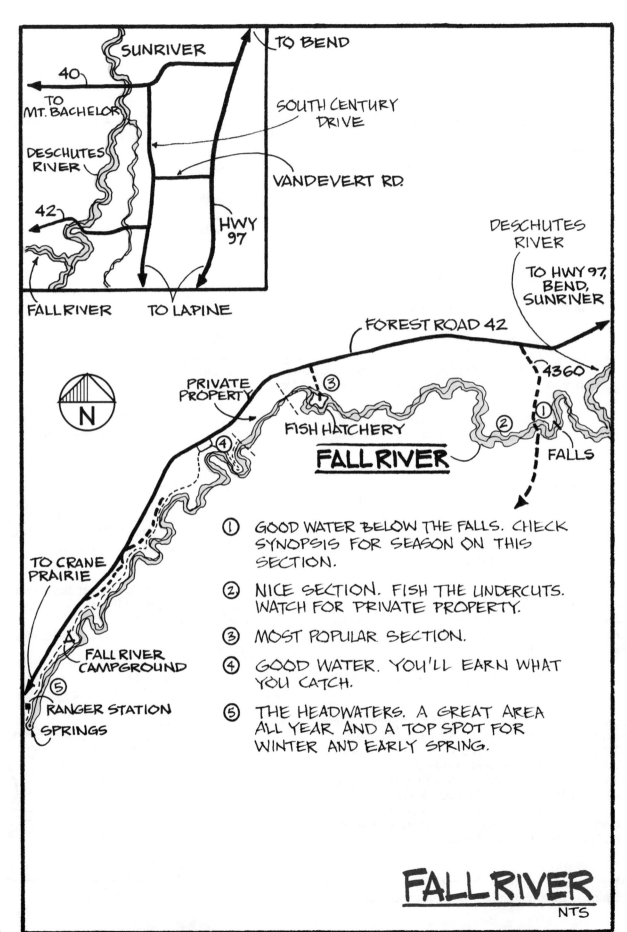

SUNRIVER

TO BEND

40

TO MT. BACHELOR

SOUTH CENTURY DRIVE

DESCHUTES RIVER

VANDEVERT RD.

42

HWY 97

FALL RIVER

TO LAPINE

DESCHUTES RIVER

TO HWY 97, BEND, SUNRIVER

FOREST ROAD 42

4360

PRIVATE PROPERTY

③

N

FISH HATCHERY

②

①

④

FALL RIVER

FALLS

TO CRANE PRAIRIE

① GOOD WATER BELOW THE FALLS. CHECK SYNOPSIS FOR SEASON ON THIS SECTION.

② NICE SECTION. FISH THE UNDERCUTS. WATCH FOR PRIVATE PROPERTY.

③ MOST POPULAR SECTION.

④ GOOD WATER. YOU'LL EARN WHAT YOU CATCH.

⑤ THE HEADWATERS. A GREAT AREA ALL YEAR AND A TOP SPOT FOR WINTER AND EARLY SPRING.

FALL RIVER CAMPGROUND

⑤

RANGER STATION

SPRINGS

FALL RIVER
NTS

Fall River

*F*all River is only about 25 miles southwest of Bend and readily accessible off Century Drive. Its proximity to the Sunriver resort and the towns of Bend and La Pine make it a popular destination for local fly fishers, especially those who prefer rivers. The water upstream from the falls is open year round which is a pleasure for winter anglers or Mt. Bachelor skiers looking for diversion from the slopes.

Fall River is approximately 10 miles long, its origin being a spring below Wickiup Reservoir. It flows through a pine forest and ultimately empties into the Deschutes River between Sunriver and La Pine. During the mosquito season, be sure to have a good repellent.

You'll like the geographic features of the area, from the gentle rolling hills of the pine forest to the volcanic cinder buttes that are scattered across the landscape. The river is very clear and cold. Good casting presentations are important. Keep a low profile along Fall River so you don't spook the fish.

Fall River has a lot of blown down timber. These logs provide cover and pools for the larger trout. Pay attention to these areas. Polarized glasses will help you spot and catch more fish in these spots. These fish are usually dining on midges and Mayflies. Caddis and small Stoneflies are also productive patterns. Weights are not permitted so use Woolly Buggers and beadhead nymphs in a dropper set up.

Type of Fish
Rainbow, brook and brown trout. The majority run 8" - 12", but keep an eye out for bigger fish.

Equipment to Use
Rods: 1 to 5 weights, 6' - 9'.
Line: Floating line to match rod weight.
Leaders: 5x to 7x, 9' - 15' depending on where you're fishing and weather.
Reels: Palm drag is fine.
Wading: Neoprene waders with felt-soled wading boots. Hippers OK on hot summer days.

Flies to Use
Dry patterns: Adams, Renegade, Comparadun, Pale Morning Dun, Blue Winged Olive, Knock Down Dun, Captive Dun, Slow Water, CDC & Elk Hair Caddis, Henryville, Griffith's Gnat, Palomino, Ant Stimulator, Humpy, Madam X, Para-hopper.
Nymphs: Pheasant Tail, Prince, Brassie, Serendipity, Hare's Ear, Sparkle Pupa, Zug Bug, Soft Hackle, also all in beadhead.
Streamers: Zonker, Woolly Bugger, Micky Finn.

When to Fish
Fishing holds up pretty well all year because of the ODFW stocking program. Most Fall River enthusiasts like late June, July and August. Evening hours generally produce the best results.

Season & Limits
Artificial flies only, weights (on line or leader) prohibited. April 26 - September 30, open below the falls. Open all year upstream from the falls. Check ODFW synopsis or a nearby fly shop for exact dates and limits.

Accommodations & Services
There are good camp sites along the river. Sunriver, Bend and La Pine have lodging and are within a half-hour drive. Stores, restaurants, gas and groceries are available in these locations.

Jeff's Opinion
This spring creek offers consistent, year around fly fishing. You'll like the beauty of the Fall River. It takes good presentation (aided by polarized glasses). If you enjoy light equipment and delicate casts, put Fall River on your "must" list.

Rating
Fall River is a high end 6.

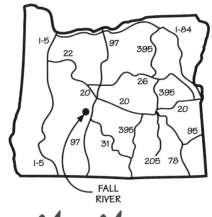

FALL RIVER

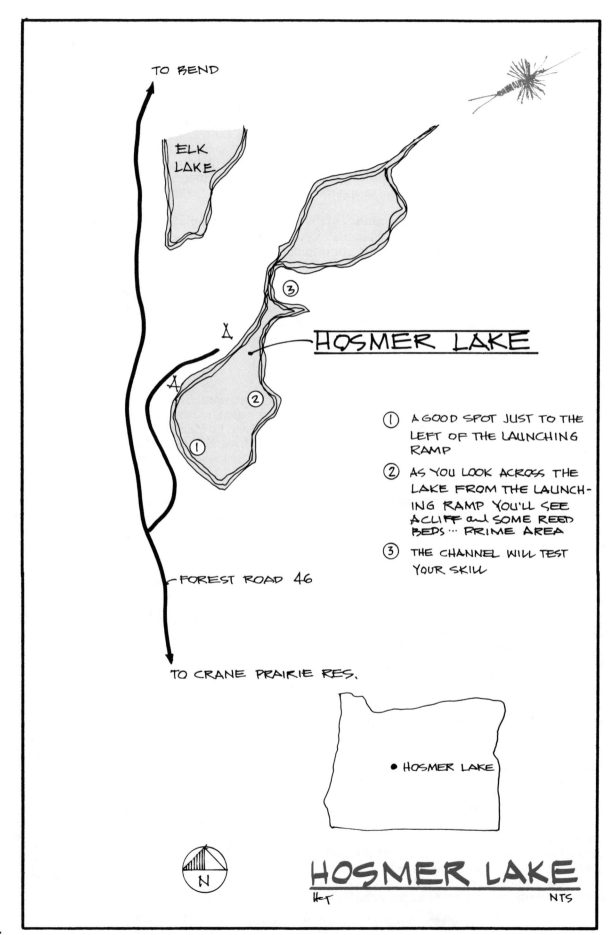

TO BEND

ELK LAKE

③

HOSMER LAKE

① A GOOD SPOT JUST TO THE LEFT OF THE LAUNCHING RAMP

② AS YOU LOOK ACROSS THE LAKE FROM THE LAUNCHING RAMP YOU'LL SEE A CLIFF and SOME REED BEDS ··· PRIME AREA

③ THE CHANNEL WILL TEST YOUR SKILL

②

①

FOREST ROAD 46

TO CRANE PRAIRIE RES.

● HOSMER LAKE

N

HOSMER LAKE
HcT   NTS

Hosmer Lake

Hosmer is one of the most unique fly-fishing-only, catch and release fisheries in the state of Oregon. Feisty landlocked Atlantic salmon and large, beautiful brook trout make this figure-eight shaped lake a real favorite of Central Oregon fly fishers.

The 6 - 20 foot deep lake has large weed beds along much of the shoreline and extensive shallows where a rich food supply helps grow the husky, good fighting fish. A shallow channel connecting the two main sections usually contains large brookies cruising the feeding lanes. Watching these fish is often as fun as figuring out how to catch them. Fish the channel, the weed beds along the west side or the east and south shores of the larger (northern) lake.

Most of Hosmer Lake can be fished from a float tube. Boats help one cover the entire area. Wading is possible, but limited due to the very soft, muddy shallows. Remember that there is no trolling, i.e. fishing from a "motor-propelled craft" when the motor is running.

Hosmer is located in Deschutes County, about 35 miles southwest of Bend, Oregon. Take Century Drive (Forest Highway 46) towards Elk Lake Resort and look for signs. Hosmer is about 10 miles from Crane Prairie Reservoir, another Central Oregon favorite.

Type of Fish
Good quality Atlantic salmon and brook trout. Both species grow to nice size in this food-rich environment.

Equipment to Use
Rods: 4 to 7 weight, 8' - 9'.
Line: Floating lines matched to rod weight.
Leaders: 4x to 6x, 9' to 15'. Fluorocarbon is great.
Reels: Mechanical and palm drag.
Wading: To fish Hosmer properly you'll need either a boat, canoe or float tube. There are restrictions on motors, so be sure to consult the ODFW synopsis. For float tubes, bring chest-high neoprene waders with felt-soled wading shoes and fins.

Flies to Use
Dry patterns: Parachute Adams, Comparadun, Parachute Caddis, Goddard Caddis, Tom Thumb, Palomino Midge, Century Drive Midge, Timberline Emerger and Callibaetis.
Nymphs: Leech, Stovepipe, Damsel, Scud, Carey Special, Beadhead Serendipity, Zug Bug, Pheasant Tail, Cates Turkey and Water Boatman.

When to Fish
It's a mixed bag of opinions. Some like June-July, while others prefer late September. I feel both are good times, with good opportunities to take nice size fish. Most all Hosmer fly fishers agree that evening is the best time of the day for any kind of fly fishing.

Season & Limits
The season opens in late April and continues through the end of October. For exact dates and limits, consult the current ODFW synopsis.

Accommodations & Services
There are good campgrounds at the lake. The nearest accommodations, food and gas are located at Elk Lake Resort, just a few miles away. A full range of services are available in Bend.

Harry's Opinion
Hosmer is a very scenic lake with lots of wildlife. If you're looking for a lake that will challenge your fly fishing skills, don't look any farther, just head for Hosmer.

Rating
A 5.5.

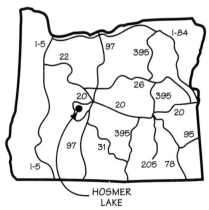

HOSMER
LAKE

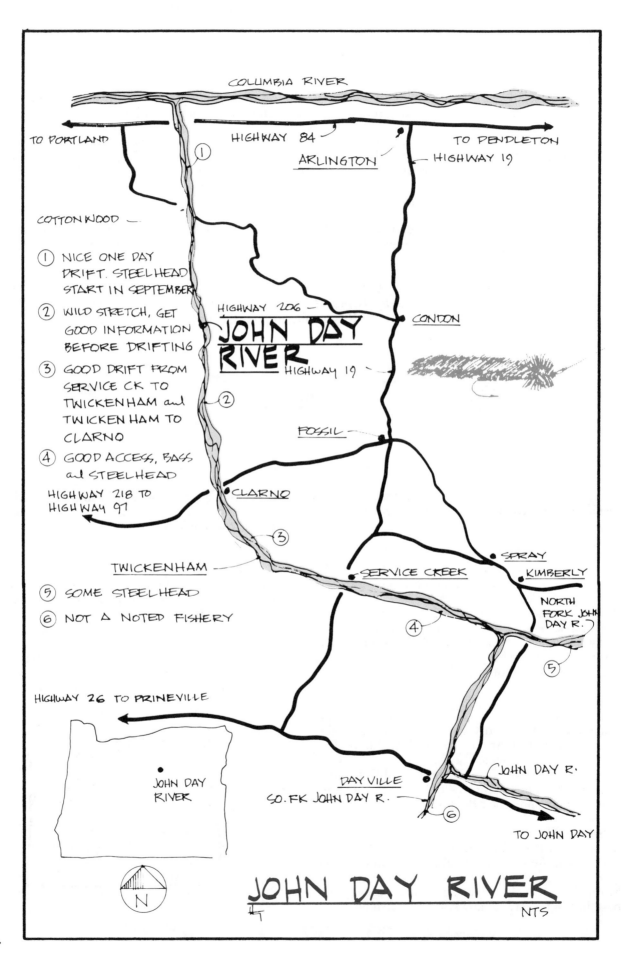

COLUMBIA RIVER

TO PORTLAND

HIGHWAY 84

ARLINGTON

TO PENDLETON

HIGHWAY 19

COTTONWOOD —

① NICE ONE DAY DRIFT. STEELHEAD START IN SEPTEMBER

② WILD STRETCH, GET GOOD INFORMATION BEFORE DRIFTING

③ GOOD DRIFT FROM SERVICE CK TO TWICKENHAM and TWICKENHAM TO CLARNO

④ GOOD ACCESS, BASS and STEELHEAD

HIGHWAY 218 TO HIGHWAY 97

HIGHWAY 206 —

JOHN DAY RIVER

HIGHWAY 19 —

CONDON

FOSSIL

CLARNO

TWICKENHAM —

⑤ SOME STEELHEAD

⑥ NOT A NOTED FISHERY

SERVICE CREEK

SPRAY

KIMBERLY

NORTH FORK JOHN DAY R.

⑤

HIGHWAY 26 TO PRINEVILLE

JOHN DAY RIVER

DAYVILLE

SO. FK JOHN DAY R. —

JOHN DAY R.

⑥

TO JOHN DAY

N

JOHN DAY RIVER

NTS

John Day River

*T*he John Day River is the only major stream in the Columbia drainage system in Oregon without a hydroelectric project blocking migratory fish. It begins in the eastern portion of Central Oregon and runs from above the town of John Day north to the Columbia River.

If you like semiarid landscape, you'll fall in love with the John Day River. There are lots of access points between Kimberly and Service Creek, but for the next 100 or so miles below Service Creek access is really limited. Drifting below Clarno can be tricky.

The John Day offers three species of fish for the fly angler. Fish for bass in the lower river spring through summer. Steelheading is good fall and winter. Trout, native and hatchery, are available most all year.

Several years ago the ODFW biologist responsible for the John Day River drainage stated that the native steelhead run in the river was the largest in Oregon. He indicated approximately 26,000 of these fish were observed on the spawning beds.

There is great variance of seasons and regulations by species and river section on the John Day. Be sure to check at a fly shop or with the ODFW in John Day (541-575-1167) for current regulations.

Type of Fish
Rainbow trout, steelhead and bass.

Equipment to Use
You'll need a variety of equipment depending on the time of year. Here are general guidelines.

Bass and Trout
Rods: 4 to 7 weight, 8' - 9'.
Line: Floating and sink tip to match rod weight.
Leaders: 3x to 5x, 7' - 9'.
Reels: Palm drag or disc drag.

Steelhead
Rods: 6 to 9 weight, 8' - 9' .
Line: Floating and sink tip to match rod weight.
Leaders: 1x to 3x, 7' - 9'.
Reels: Mechanical drag.
Wading: Chest-high neoprenes with felt-soled wading shoes or stream cleats and a wading staff. If you are planning to float below Clarno, consult a qualified and knowledgeable guide.

Flies to Use
This is tough since you can fish for trout, bass and steelhead. My experience suggests the following:
Dry patterns: Adams, Renegade, Elk Horn Caddis, X Caddis, Humpy, Lt. Cahill, Blue Winged Olive, Comparadun, Grasshopper, Foam Ant.
Nymphs & streamers: Woolly Worm, Hare's Ear, Matuka, Muddler, Zonker, Woolly Buggers.
Steelhead: Skunks, Green Butted Skunk, Red Wing Blackbird and Silver Hilton.
Bass: Surface poppers, sliders and wiggle bugs are effective and fun. Try yellow and chartreuse first, then orange, red, white, black, brown, green and purple.

When to Fish
Water flows vary dramatically. I suggest you consult a qualified guide. Fish for bass May - August, steelhead late fall and winter months.

Season & Limits
Regulations vary on this river system, so it's important to refer to the ODFW synopsis for current regulations.

Accommodations & Services
Facilities are limited along the accessible length of the river. Restaurants, service stations and groceries are downstream from Kimberly. There are some nice camp sites between Kimberly and Service Creek.

Harry's Opinion
The John Day can range from a 2 to a 6 depending on when you fish. I suggest you take the time to carefully evaluate the steelhead fishery.

Rating
For trout a 2. For bass an 8. Steelhead, a strong 5.

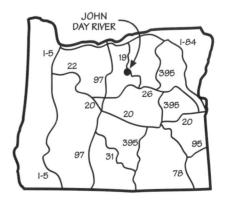

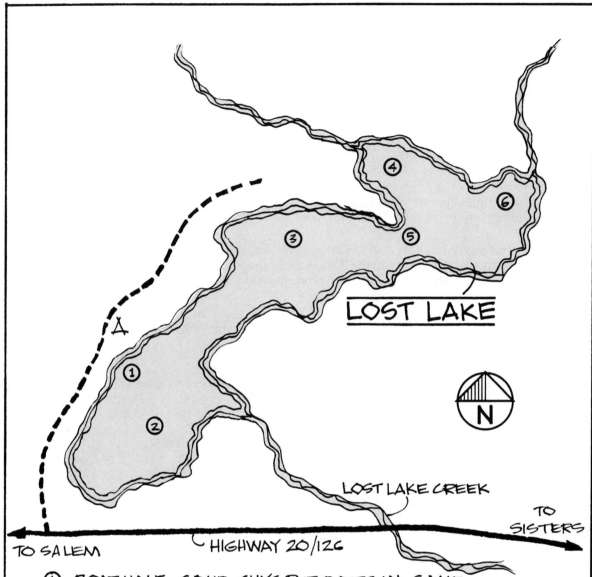

LOST LAKE

LOST LAKE CREEK

TO SISTERS

TO SALEM

HIGHWAY 20/126

① BOAT HOLE - SOME GUYS PUT BOATS IN, SOME GUYS CATCH FISH.

② HIGHWAY HOLE - NICE SPOT IN THE EARLY SEASON. USE FLOAT TUBE OR BOAT.

③ SPRING HOLE - A "SAVE THE DAY" SPOT DURING HOT WEATHER.

④ BAY OF PIGS - GOOD AREA TO FIND FISH FEEDING ON OR NEAR THE SURFACE.

⑤ THE POINT - IF YOU ARE WADING, THIS IS THE PLACE.

⑥ OSPREY POINT - A FINE SPOT FOR TROLLING JUST OUT FROM THE SHORELINE.

LOST LAKE

NTS

Lost Lake

Here's an excellent stillwater fishery very near Sisters, Black Butte Ranch and Camp Sherman, and hardly anyone talks about it. Lost Lake is very easy to locate and great for float tubing. If you can get over the occasional traffic noise from the highway, you'll enjoy casting to lots of healthy trout in one of the most productive lakes in the Sisters area.

Situated in a basin below Three Fingered Jack mountain, this 50 acre natural lake is fed by snow runoff and springs that well up from below the lake's surface. The lake is shallow, with lots of prime habitat for fish and insects. The weedbeds are full of nymphs, including Callibaetis, gray drake, damsel, dragonflies, chironomids and numerous stillwater dwelling caddis. Add in the abundant leech and scud populations and you can see why the rainbow and Brookies grow fat here.

Spring and early summer are the best times to fish Lost Lake. By late summer the lake gets very low (at the highway end) yet has decent water towards the back. This low water period is a good time to wade the many shallow areas. Most of the year, however, a float tube or pram is the best way to reach the fish.

Lost Lake can be found by driving west of Sisters on Highway 20 about 28 miles. It is about 2 miles from Santiam Junction and is easily accessible from Salem, Eugene and Corvallis, making it a popular destination for Oregon fly fishers.

Type of Fish
Rainbow and brook trout.

Known Hatches
Callibaetis, Gray Drakes, midges, damsels, dragon-flies, Longhorned Caddis, Traveling Sedge, and Flying Ants. Also important, leech, scud, waterboatman and snail.

Equipment to Use
Rods: 4 or 5 weight 8 1/2' - 10'.
Line: Floating, intermediate and type II full sink.
Leaders: 4x - 6x, 9' to 15'. 7 1/2' on sinking lines.
Reels: Click or disc drag.
Wading / Tubing: Neoprene waders early in the season, lightweight waders July - Sept. Felt-soled boots. Many Lost Lake regulars use a kick-boat with small oars.

Flies to Use
Dries: Callibaetis Parachute and Spinner, Adams Parachute, Comparadun, Timberline Emerger, Captive Dun, Suspender Midge, Griffith's Gnat, Para-midge, Adult Damsel, Black Elk Hair Caddis, Tom Thumb, Goddard Caddis, X Caddis, Ant, Red Tarantula, Float-n-Fool.
Nymphs: Beadhead Leeches (black, olive, red, yellow, rust), Woolly Bugger, Scud, Waterboatman, Borger's Snail, Prince, Pheasant Tail, Olive Flashback Hare's Ear, Bloodworm, Carey Specials, Damsel, Sparkle Pupa, Soft Hackle Hare's Ear, large Gold-Ribbed Hare's Ears.

When to Fish
At over 4,500 foot elevation, on Santiam Pass, Lost Lake can remain frozen and snowbound until May. Fishing is usually good in May after ice-out. June and July are the best months, but don't overlook the rest of the season, especially evenings.

Seasons & Regulations
The lake is open all year. Ice coverage dictates when you can fish. Catch & release and barbless flies or lures are the law.

Accommodations & Services
All services are available in Sisters. There is a campground at the lake.

Jeff's Opinion
Not a Blue Ribbon fishery but a great locals hangout, favorite tubing lake and worth fishing for nice trout.

Rating
A good 6.

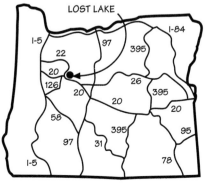

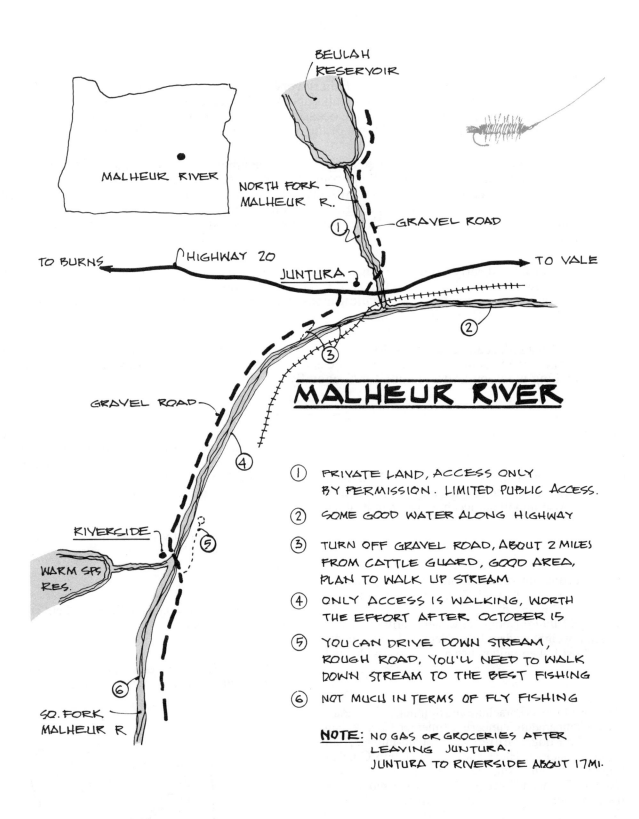

BEULAH RESERVOIR

MALHEUR RIVER

NORTH FORK MALHEUR R.

GRAVEL ROAD

TO BURNS ← HIGHWAY 20

JUNTURA

TO VALE →

① ② ③

MALHEUR RIVER

GRAVEL ROAD

④

RIVERSIDE

WARM SPS RES.

⑤

⑥

SO. FORK MALHEUR R

① PRIVATE LAND, ACCESS ONLY BY PERMISSION. LIMITED PUBLIC ACCESS.

② SOME GOOD WATER ALONG HIGHWAY

③ TURN OFF GRAVEL ROAD, ABOUT 2 MILES FROM CATTLE GUARD, GOOD AREA, PLAN TO WALK UP STREAM

④ ONLY ACCESS IS WALKING, WORTH THE EFFORT AFTER OCTOBER 15

⑤ YOU CAN DRIVE DOWN STREAM, ROUGH ROAD, YOU'LL NEED TO WALK DOWN STREAM TO THE BEST FISHING

⑥ NOT MUCH IN TERMS OF FLY FISHING

NOTE: NO GAS OR GROCERIES AFTER LEAVING JUNTURA. JUNTURA TO RIVERSIDE ABOUT 17MI.

N

MALHEUR RIVER
HLT   NTS

Malheur River

*T*he main stem of the Malheur and the North Fork of the Malheur offer some of the finest fall trout fishing I've ever experienced. I like to fly fish the main river from Riverside to about 10 miles below Juntura. I fish the North Fork above Beulah Reservoir.

The fishing in the main river is far and away the best from mid-October (after the irrigation season) until the winter weather makes you seek a warm fire and a good book. You can fish the North Fork nearly anytime, but it will require some fairly strenuous walking.

The area of the main Malheur, where I fish and what we describe in this guide, is about 65 miles east of Burns on Highway 20. As a matter of interest, the headwaters of the Malheur is in the Strawberry Range and flows into the Snake River on the Oregon-Idaho border.

Because of high and turbid water conditions, there is little reason for the fly fisher to venture to the main stem of the Malheur during the spring and summer. Late fall is another story. I can't think of a place I'd rather be than on the Malheur.

Type of Fish
The Malheur is primarily a rainbow fishery.

Equipment to Use
You don't have to be very sophisticated on the Malheur.
Rods: 3 to 6 weight.
Line: Floating line to match rod weight.
Leaders: 4x, 5x and 6x, 9'.
Reels: Palm drag.
Wading: Lots of walking here, so use "light" wading equipment. Hip boots are fine, or simply wear wading shoes and light weight pants.

Flies to Use
Dry patterns: Hopper, Royal Wulff, Olive and Rusty Spinners, Comparadun, Renegade, Adams, Elk Hair Caddis.
Nymphs: Hare's Ear, Prince and Pheasant Tail.
Streamers: Woolly Worm, Muddler and Sculpin.

When to Fish
The quality fishing on the Malheur is usually after October 15. This is when the river ceases to be an irrigation conduit for the rich farm land of the Treasure Valley.

Season & Limits
The Malheur River is open all year; however, regulations and limits are subject to change, so refer to the ODFW synopsis for current information.

Accommodations & Services
There are limited facilities in the fishable area of the Malheur. Juntura has a motel and restaurant.

Harry's Opinion
I've spent many wonderful fall days on the Malheur with my wife and friends. We mostly fish, but we also hunt chukar. If you're looking for a place to spend a delightful fall, both fly fishing and bird hunting, take a fling at the Malheur between Riverside and Juntura.

Rating
The Malheur, in the fall or spring when the water is right, is a 7. During the summer, when it's an irrigation conduit, it's a 1.

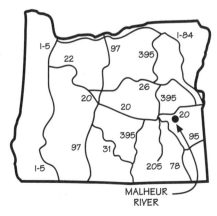

MALHEUR RIVER

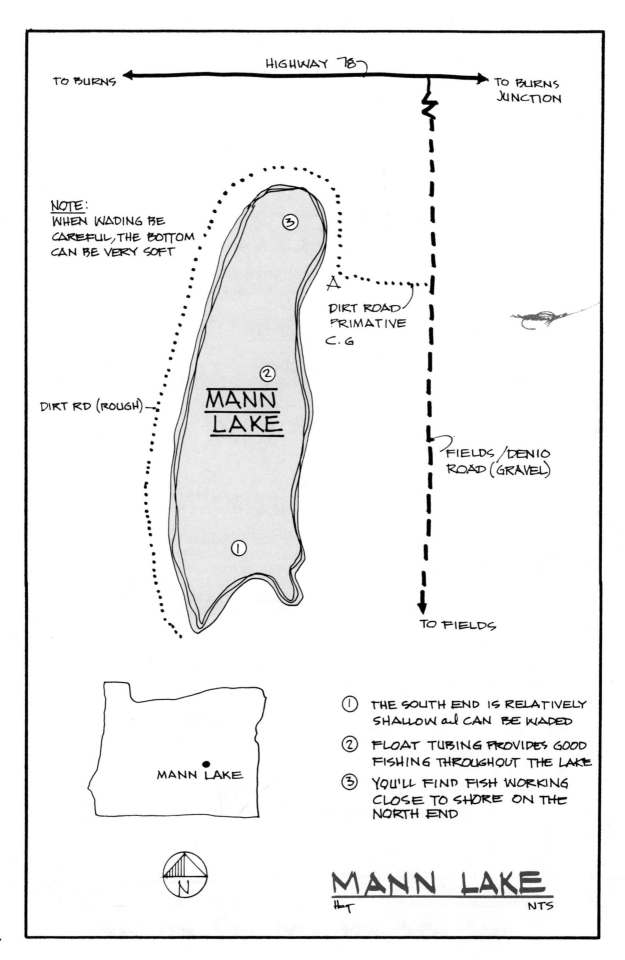

HIGHWAY 78

TO BURNS

TO BURNS JUNCTION

NOTE:
WHEN WADING BE CAREFUL, THE BOTTOM CAN BE VERY SOFT

③

Ⓐ

DIRT ROAD PRIMITIVE C.G

② MANN LAKE

DIRT RD (ROUGH)

FIELDS / DENIO ROAD (GRAVEL)

①

TO FIELDS

MANN LAKE

① THE SOUTH END IS RELATIVELY SHALLOW and CAN BE WADED

② FLOAT TUBING PROVIDES GOOD FISHING THROUGHOUT THE LAKE

③ YOU'LL FIND FISH WORKING CLOSE TO SHORE ON THE NORTH END

N

MANN LAKE

HaT   NTS

Mann Lake

*M*ann Lake is remote. If there is such a thing as a pure desert lake, this is it. With the Steens Mountain as a backdrop, and the desert floor as a stage, Mann Lake will dazzle you with exceptional desert scenery and good size fish. It's roughly 270 acres in size (may vary with precipitation) which is large enough for elbow room.

Mann Lake lies on the east side of the Steens Mountain. Take Highway 78 out of Burns and turn south on the Fields-Denio Road (some maps call it Folly Farm Road). This is a good gravel road. From the turnoff on Highway 78 it's about 35 miles to Mann Lake.

Type of Fish
Cutthroat from 12" to 20", with some a little larger.

Equipment to Use
Rods: 4 to 7 weight depending on the weather.
Line: Floating line to match rod weight.
Leaders: 3x, 4x and 5x, 9'.
Reels: Palm and mechanical drag.
Wading: It is possible to get to fish by wading the lake, but it's hard. Mann Lake's bottom is very soft and in some areas you're in muck up to your knees. The best way to fish Mann is from a float tube; the choice of most experienced Mann Lake fly fishers. Boats and canoes are also used.

Flies to Use
You'll have the best results on Mann Lake using nymphs and streamers: Zug Bug, Woolly Bugger, Leech, Damsel, Prince and Zonker. Fishing on the lake is restricted to barbless flies and lures.

When to Fish
As soon as the ice is off the lake in the spring, things start to happen. This action continues until the water warms in July and August. Good fishing starts again in late September and October. The time of day doesn't seem to make that much difference.

Season & Limits
Mann Lake is open year around. All fish under 16" must be returned to the lake unharmed. The limit is 2 fish over 16". Since regulations are subject to change, refer to the ODFW synopsis for current regulations.

Accommodations & Services
This is very simple: there are not any accommodations or services within 50 miles of the lake. The campground on the north end of the lake is unimproved and drinking water is not available. If you need something, you'll have to travel about 50 miles south to Fields (they have great hamburgers at Fields) or the Princeton/Crane area or return to Burns. The gravel roads in this area are well maintained but have a reputation as tire eaters. Several years ago, I had two blowouts in 35 miles. That takes a lot of fun out of the day. Be sure your gas tank and water containers are full before departing for Mann Lake.

Harry's Opinion
If you haven't experienced fly fishing a desert lake, try Mann. In the spring and fall, Mann is an exceptional fishery. Word of warning: wind. There are times when the wind prevents fly fishing and forces you to park your car on top of your tent to keep it from blowing into Idaho.

Rating
A very solid 6.5.

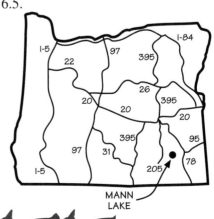

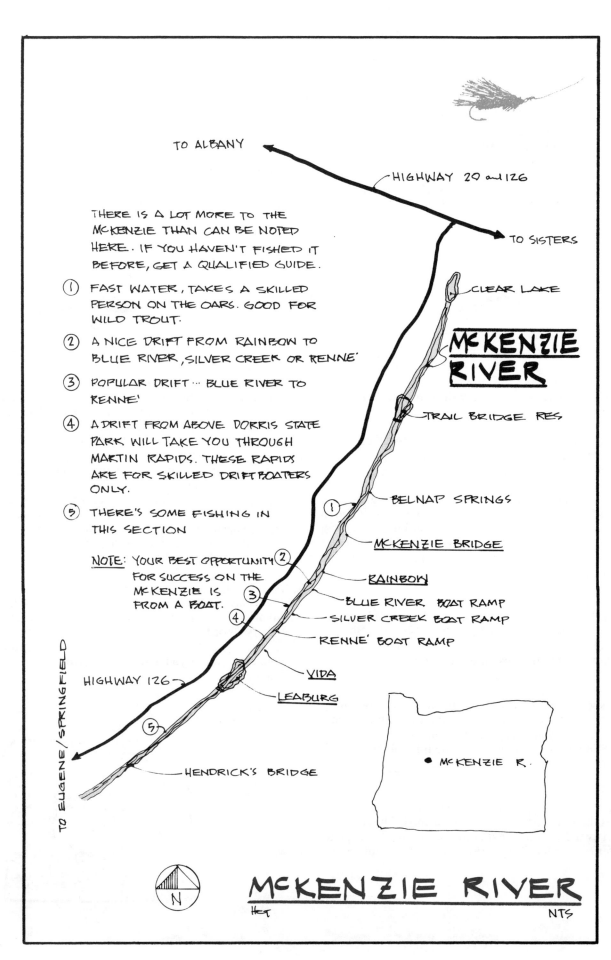

TO ALBANY

HIGHWAY 20 and 126

TO SISTERS

THERE IS A LOT MORE TO THE MCKENZIE THAN CAN BE NOTED HERE. IF YOU HAVEN'T FISHED IT BEFORE, GET A QUALIFIED GUIDE.

① FAST WATER, TAKES A SKILLED PERSON ON THE OARS. GOOD FOR WILD TROUT.

② A NICE DRIFT FROM RAINBOW TO BLUE RIVER, SILVER CREEK OR RENNE'

③ POPULAR DRIFT ··· BLUE RIVER TO RENNE'

④ A DRIFT FROM ABOVE DORRIS STATE PARK WILL TAKE YOU THROUGH MARTIN RAPIDS. THESE RAPIDS ARE FOR SKILLED DRIFT BOATERS ONLY.

⑤ THERE'S SOME FISHING IN THIS SECTION

NOTE: YOUR BEST OPPORTUNITY FOR SUCCESS ON THE MCKENZIE IS FROM A BOAT.

CLEAR LAKE

McKENZIE RIVER

TRAIL BRIDGE RES.

BELNAP SPRINGS

McKENZIE BRIDGE

RAINBOW

BLUE RIVER BOAT RAMP

SILVER CREEK BOAT RAMP

RENNE' BOAT RAMP

VIDA

HIGHWAY 126

LEABURG

TO EUGENE / SPRINGFIELD

HENDRICK'S BRIDGE

McKENZIE R.

N

HCJ

McKENZIE RIVER

NTS

McKenzie River

*T*he McKenzie is one of the most beautiful rivers in the west. The McKenzie drift boat originated on this river, a boat type which is now used worldwide. President Hoover spent much of his fishing life on the McKenzie, but so have a lot of other people. There are numerous good resorts and motels located on or adjacent to the river. A night or two in these comfortable lodgings, coupled with a guided fly fishing drift, is one of the better recreational investments you'll make.

Rainbow trout, steelhead and salmon call the McKenzie home. For trout anglers, the McKenzie has hatches of caddis, mayflies, some stones and terrestrials. When the season opens in late April, the dry fly activity is just starting. For salmon and steelhead, the season is generally best winter-spring and downstream of Leaburg Dam and the town of Vida.

From Central Oregon, travel west of Sisters on Highway 26 about 50 miles and you will come to the best fishing section on the McKenzie. Highway 26 parallels the river from its source at Clear Lake to Eugene.

Type of Fish
There are two types of rainbows: stocked and native. The native fish are referred to as Redsides. The stocked fish (the majority) run from 8" to 12". The Redsides range from 12" to 20".

Equipment to Use
Rods: 5, 6 and 7 weight, 8-9'.
Line: For trout, either a floating or sink tip line will serve you, though you'll probably use your floating line the majority of the time.
Leader: When fishing dry, 4x - 5x, 9'. For nymphs use a strike indicator.
Reels: Mechanical and palm drag.
Wading: Not many good areas. They are isolated and one must search for them. Best to drift this stream.

Flies to Use
Dry patterns: Adams, Renegade, Stimulator, Henryville, Light Cahill, Flying Ant, Royal Wulff, Humpy, Elk Hair Caddis and Comparadun. I've seen October Caddis patterns work well.
Nymphs: Prince, Hare's Ear, Sparkle Pupa, Black Woolly Bugger, Pheasant Tail.
Steelhead: Skunks, Green Butted Skunk, Silver Hilton.

When to Fish
The heavyweight guides like the river best from late May to early September. You can generally catch fish all day long because there are always some sections of the river in shadow.

Seasons & Limits
The upper river is open from late April to the end of October. Parts of the lower river are open year around. For exact dates and limits, check the ODFW synopsis.

Accommodations & Services
Stores, restaurants and gas stations are located from McKenzie Bridge to Walterville. For those not fishing, there's excellent golf nearby at the Tokatee Golf Club.

Where to Fish
The McKenzie has limited access, due to private property and a very difficult shoreline to wade. I suggest you retain the services of a qualified McKenzie River guide.

Harry's Opinion
For sheer fishing pleasure, on one of the West's most notable streams, the McKenzie offers one of life's great rewards. But, as I said, go with a qualified guide.

Rating
The McKenzie River, with a guide, is a strong 7.

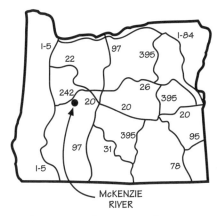

McKENZIE RIVER

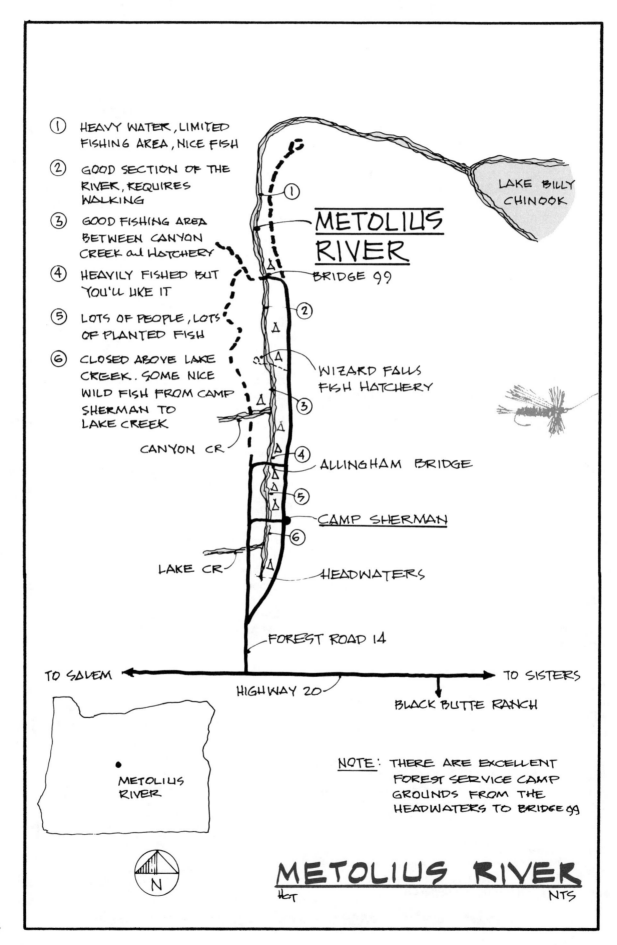

① HEAVY WATER, LIMITED FISHING AREA, NICE FISH

② GOOD SECTION OF THE RIVER, REQUIRES WALKING

③ GOOD FISHING AREA BETWEEN CANYON CREEK and Hatchery

④ HEAVILY FISHED BUT YOU'LL LIKE IT

⑤ LOTS OF PEOPLE, LOTS OF PLANTED FISH

⑥ CLOSED ABOVE LAKE CREEK. SOME NICE WILD FISH FROM CAMP SHERMAN TO LAKE CREEK

LAKE BILLY CHINOOK

METOLIUS RIVER

BRIDGE 99

WIZARD FALLS FISH HATCHERY

CANYON CR

ALLINGHAM BRIDGE

CAMP SHERMAN

LAKE CR

HEADWATERS

FOREST ROAD 14

TO SALEM

HIGHWAY 20

TO SISTERS

BLACK BUTTE RANCH

METOLIUS RIVER

NOTE: THERE ARE EXCELLENT FOREST SERVICE CAMP GROUNDS FROM THE HEADWATERS TO BRIDGE 99

N

METOLIUS RIVER

HGT

NTS

Metolius River

*T*he Metolius, approximately 15 miles north and west of Sisters off Highway 20, flows through a beautiful setting of old-growth pine forests with spectacular mountain views. The camping facilities are excellent and help make this a wonderful family recreation area.

In August of 1995 the Metolius went to wild fish only and all stocking was halted. This, along with some regulation changes, has been a very positive change. As of this writing, all trout fishing is catch & release with barbless hooks, *only*. No weight of any kind is allowed on your line or leader. Use weighted flies for nymphing.

Trout here often don't rise like fish in other rivers, so it's important to fool them with patterns they perceive to be an easy meal. The Metolius has an assortment of hatches daily and throughout the year including stones, caddis, mayflies, midges and terrestrials. In general, mayflies hatch year-round and caddis hatch from early spring to late fall. The evening caddis emergence is best in summer. Late June - September Stonefly hatches on the Metolius are amazing. You should also experiment with transitional or crippled dry fly patterns.

The Metolius is a fine fishing resource. It's crystal clear waters are tricky and it will take you some time to learn the river's idiosyncrasies, so be realistic with your expectations.

I recommend a visit to the headwaters of the Metolius. This site offers one of the most beautiful scenes in the Northwest. The river starts from springs near the base of Black Butte. The view of snowclad Mt. Jefferson, from across the meadow and river, is spectacular.

Type of Fish
Predominantly rainbows, some brown trout and whitefish, 11" - 18". Also bull trout, that can get to 15 pounds, but average 3 to 5 lbs.

Equipment to Use
Rods: 1 to 7 weight, 6 1/2' - 9'.
Line: Floating line is best. For Bull trout, use a sink tip.
Leaders: 5x to 7x, 12' - 18' for dry. 9' to 12', strike indicator for wet or nymph fishing.
Reels: Click or disc drag is fine.
Wading: Chest-high neoprenes, felt-soled boots.

Flies to Use
Dry patterns: Sparkle, Captive & Knock Down Dun, Comparadun, Thorax Ties and Spinners to match Baetis, Pale Morning Dun, Green Drake, Cinygmula, Mahogany Dun, Pale Evening Dun and Flav's. Elk Hair, CDC, Parachute, Henryville, Slow Water and X Caddis. Clark's Stone, Sofa Pillow, Stimulator, Yellow Sally, Olive CDC, Parachute Adams.
Nymphs: Beadhead Pheasant Tail, Prince or Flashback. Hare's Ear, Zug Bug, Golden Stone, October Caddis, Soft Hackles, Brassie.
Streamers: Sculpin, Zonker, White Rabbit Leech.

When to Fish
The river fishes pretty well year around. Move up and down stream to find feeding fish. There can be excellent action November through March. I've never found the Metolius to be an early morning stream. Best results seem to be after 9:30 AM.

Seasons & Limits
Fly fishing only from Bridge 99 upstream to the private property boundary near the walk-in campgrounds. Winter, fly fishing only below Allingham Bridge. No boats or tubes. Check at a fly shop or the ODFW synopsis for areas with special regulations.

Accommodations & Services
Very good lodging, restaurants, and stores at Camp Sherman, Black Butte Ranch and Sisters.

Harry & Jeff's Opinion
One of our favorites. A challenging river for mid to expert fly fishing abilities. Learn it, protect it and enjoy it. A gem by any standards.

Rating
The Metolius is a strong 6.

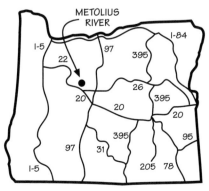

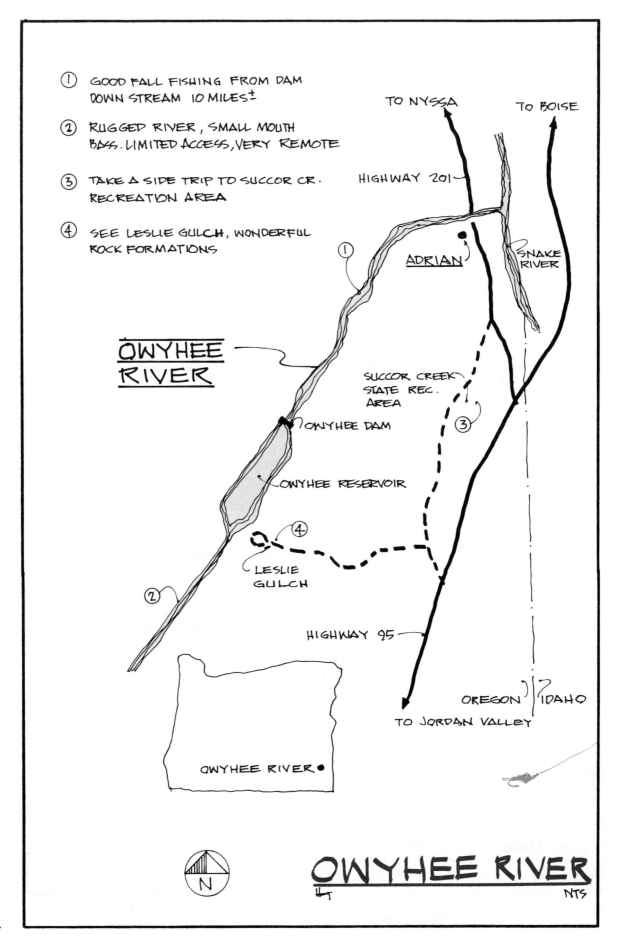

① GOOD FALL FISHING FROM DAM DOWN STREAM 10 MILES±

② RUGGED RIVER, SMALL MOUTH BASS. LIMITED ACCESS, VERY REMOTE

③ TAKE A SIDE TRIP TO SUCCOR CR. RECREATION AREA

④ SEE LESLIE GULCH, WONDERFUL ROCK FORMATIONS

TO NYSSA

TO BOISE

HIGHWAY 201

ADRIAN

SNAKE RIVER

OWYHEE RIVER

SUCCOR CREEK STATE REC. AREA

OWYHEE DAM

OWYHEE RESERVOIR

LESLIE GULCH

HIGHWAY 95

OREGON | IDAHO

TO JORDAN VALLEY

OWYHEE RIVER●

N

OWYHEE RIVER

NTS

Owyhee River

*T*he Owyhee River (pronounced Oh-wa-hee) runs easterly from its source in Nevada towards the town of Adrian and then flows into the Snake River. The only part of the Owyhee River I'll address here is the part of the river flowing from the Owyhee Dam downstream about 10 miles.

The geological formations along this river section are fantastic. Rock formations and colors are stunning, to say the least. Even if you don't fish, the trip up the Owyhee River to the dam and Lake Owyhee is worth your time. In the fall, you can combine fishing with chukar hunting. You'll find plenty of both. The river is always off color (milky) but don't let that bother you. It's very fishable.

Type of Fish
Rainbows from 7" to 15". This is also known as a good brown trout fishery.

Equipment to Use
The Owyhee is a fairly good-sized river and long casts are sometimes needed.
Rods: 4 to 7 weight, 8' - 9'.
Line: Floating line to match rod weight.
Leaders: 4x and 5x, 9'.
Reels: Palm drag is fine.
Wading: Waist-high or chest-high neoprenes and felt-soled wading shoes. Always carry a wading staff. It helps you probe the bottom in the off-colored water. Wade with care.

Flies to Use
There are hatches of midges, caddis and mayflies during the spring, summer and fall. My experience is that small patterns produce the best results.
Dry patterns: Adams, Captive Dun, Elk Hair Caddis, Comparadun, Pale Morning Dun, Rusty, Olive and Black Spinners, Blue Winged Olive, Renegade (#16 and #18), X Caddis, Slow Water Caddis.
Nymphs: Hare's Ear, Midge Pupa, Beadhead Pheasant Tail, Scud, Sparkle Pupa, Beadhead Serendipity, Prince and Chironomid Pupa.
Streamers: Zonker, Woolly Buggers, Marabou Muddlers.

When to Fish
I like the fall, mid-September through October. The fish are active on the surface and are eager to attack most anything that is properly presented. Fishing is good all day. It doesn't appear that one time is any better than another. I favor afternoon and evening fishing.

Season & Limits
The Owyhee below the dam is open year-round and has been catch and release only for browns. This can change so check at a fly shop and consult the current ODFW synopsis for seasons and limits.

Accommodations & Services
There are a lot of good campsites along the river. Most are unimproved. Overnight accommodations, restaurants, gas and groceries are available in Adrain, Nyssa and at the resort on Lake Owyhee.

Harry's Opinion
The Owyhee River is a great place to spend time in the fall. The fishing can be very good. It's picturesque and there is plenty of sight-seeing in the area. While you are there, you should take the drive through the Succor Creek State Recreational Area and Leslie Gulch. These areas have exceptionally beautiful rock formations, canyons and other geologic features.

Rating
The Owyhee rates a soft 5. Devoted Owyhee fly fishers won't agree with this low rating.

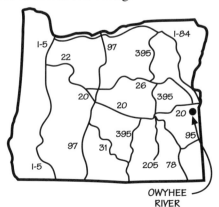

OWYHEE RIVER

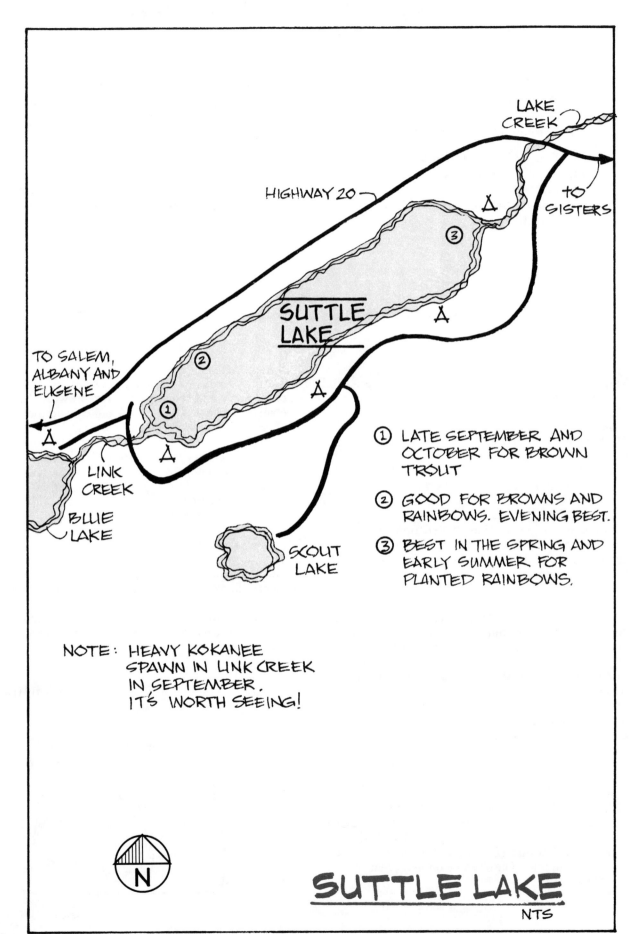

Suttle Lake

*T*his large lake is about 15 miles west of Sisters on the south side of Highway 20. The lake is surrounded by pine forest and there are some excellent views of the nearby Cascade Mountains.

When a lake is this easy to get to, you wouldn't expect it to have a good population of large brown trout. Suttle has them, nonetheless, and they can be taken with flies. You'll also find rainbow trout and a strong population of kokanee (landlocked salmon). Browns will be from 1 to 5 pounds. A few are bigger. Rainbows are planted and average from 8" to 12". Kokanee will be in the 9" to 14" range.

There are only a few good places one can wade to fish, most notably near the boat ramp and Link Creek. A float tube is a good way to cover a lot of area with a fly rod. Most people fish Suttle Lake from a boat.

Suttle Lake is one of the better family lakes in the region with excellent campgrounds and boat launching ramps. There are a lot of recreational activities available around Suttle Lake; horseback riding, hiking and water skiing to name a few.

Type of Fish
Wild brown trout, hatchery rainbows and kokanee salmon.

Equipment to Use
Rods: 5, 6 or 7 weight, 8 - 91/2'.
Line: Floating and sink tip for flexibility.
Leaders: 3x, 4x and 5x, 9'.
Reels: Mechanical and palm drag.
Wading: Chest-high, neoprene waders and felt-soled wading boots. Float tubing is a good Suttle fly fishing method. You'll need the above wading equipment for tubing, along with a pair of fins.

Flies to Use
As you would expect, fly patterns will change depending on the time of year you're fishing Suttle. Ask around or at a local fly shop.
Dry patterns: Renegade, Adams, Royal Wulff, Comparadun.
Nymphs and Streamers: Hare's Ear, Prince, Carey Special, Zonker, Muddler, Woolly Bugger.

When to Fish
You'll find the best fishing in May and June and again in late September and October. For browns, it's best late in the year, with late afternoon and evening being most productive. Generally, there aren't any water skiers during these latter time periods.

Season & Limits
Suttle opens in late April and closes the end of October. Limits vary from 5 trout per day to 20 kokanee per day and are subject to change, so consult a fly shop or the ODFW synopsis for exact dates and bag limits.

Accommodations & Services
There are campgrounds on the south side and the west end of the lake. A store and restaurant are located on the west end. A store, restaurant and small dock sit on the east end of the lake near a beach and group picnic shelter. There are overnight accommodations, restaurants, gas and groceries in Sisters, Camp Sherman and Black Butte Ranch.

Harry's Opinion
If you're looking for an easy access lake with better than average fishing, Suttle is a good choice. It may be the most underrated lake in Central Oregon.

Rating
Suttle, for overall fishing is a 6.5. For fly fishing it's a soft 5.

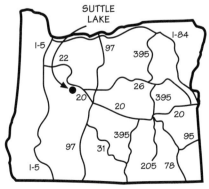

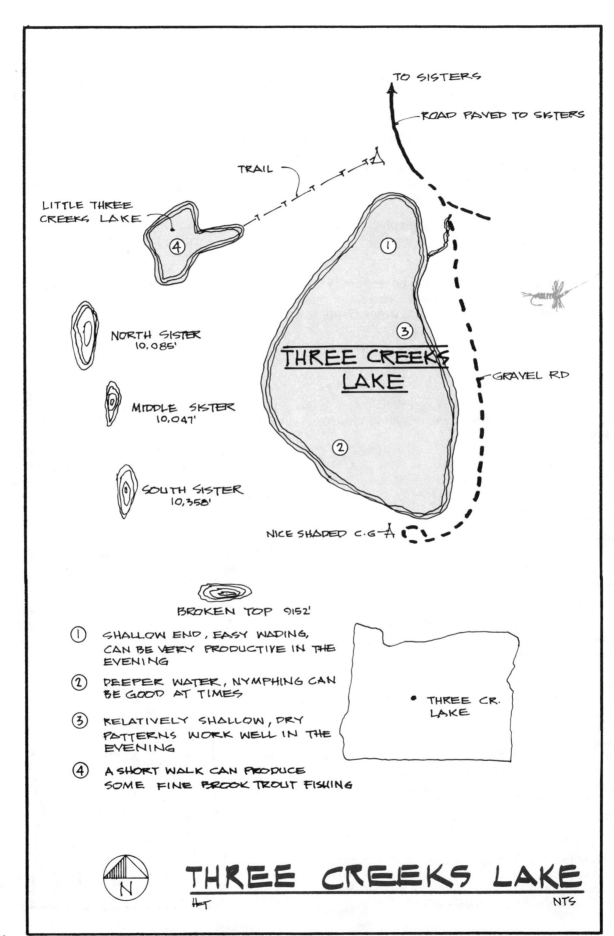

TO SISTERS

ROAD PAVED TO SISTERS

TRAIL

LITTLE THREE
CREEKS LAKE

④

① THREE CREEKS
LAKE

③

GRAVEL RD

NORTH SISTER
10,085'

MIDDLE SISTER
10,047'

SOUTH SISTER
10,358'

②

NICE SHADED C.G

BROKEN TOP 9152'

① SHALLOW END, EASY WADING,
CAN BE VERY PRODUCTIVE IN THE
EVENING

② DEEPER WATER, NYMPHING CAN
BE GOOD AT TIMES

③ RELATIVELY SHALLOW, DRY
PATTERNS WORK WELL IN THE
EVENING

④ A SHORT WALK CAN PRODUCE
SOME FINE BROOK TROUT FISHING

• THREE CR.
LAKE

N

THREE CREEKS LAKE

H+T

NTS

Three Creeks Lake

*P*robably the majority of the traffic going the 18 miles (from Sisters) to Three Creeks Lake is headed for a hike into the scenic Three Sisters Wilderness. There aren't many people headed up there packing fly rods. Just going up to Three Creeks Lake is well worth the trip.

South of Sisters, at the base of Broken Top and the Three Sisters Mountains, lie 30 acre Three Creeks and 14 acre Little Three Creeks Lakes. The bigger lake and smaller cousin are in a beautiful high Cascade, alpine setting at approximately 6,500. Here is a fishing trip that's worth the ride for the scenic value alone. Besides the scenery, odds are in your favor that you'll catch some fish.

Float tubing is a good way to fish the lakes. Cast dry flies if you see a hatch, otherwise sink nymphs and retrieve slowly. If you prefer a boat, or if you have small children, that's OK too but you must row or paddle. Motors are NOT allowed on Three Creeks, or Little Three Creeks Lakes. Float tube enthusiasts should note that to get to Little Three Creeks Lake (from the bigger lake) requires about a mile hike from the Driftwood camp ground. Or, it's a 40 minute hike in from the meadow trailhead.

The easiest way to get to the lakes is from downtown Sisters. Take Elm street south. This road (also Forest Service Road 16) is closed in winter about 15 miles from town. Fishing the lakes usually starts in late May depending on snow pack.

Type of Fish
Three Creeks Lake has both rainbow and brook trout that run from 8" to 15". Little Three Creeks Lake has a good population of self propagating brook trout that will go to about 14". The little lake also has some stocked rainbows in the 12" range and a few larger rainbow that manage to hold over from winter to winter.

Equipment to Use
Rods: 3 to 7 weight.
Line: Floating line to match rod weight. Some fly fishers like to use sink tip line, though I haven't found it that necessary.
Leaders: 4x and 5x, 9'.
Reels: Palm drag is adequate.
Wading: There are parts of the lake you can wade. You'll need chest-high waders and wading boots. Float tubes are a good idea.

Flies to Use
Dry patterns: Adams, Renegade, Elk Hair Caddis, Comparadun, Ant and Royal Wulff.
Nymphs: Hare's Ear, Polly Casual Dress, Pheasant Tail, Damsel and Chironomid.

When to Fish
July, August, September and October are regarded as the best months. The evening hours have the best fly fishing.

Season & Limits
The season opens in late April and closes the end of October. For limits and exact dates, refer to local fly shops or the ODFW synopsis.

Accommodations & Services
There are two very nice campgrounds and a seasonal store with boat rentals and small dock at Three Creeks Lake. All other services are available in Sisters. Little Three Creeks Lake is a hike-in or pack-in lake. There are no official campgrounds or other services at the little lake.

Harry & Jeff's Opinion
These lake are fun to fish, especially with a float tube.

Rating
Three Creeks and Little Three Creeks are soft 5's.

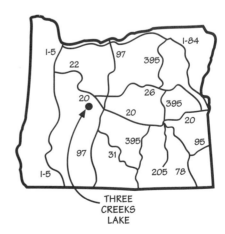

THREE
CREEKS
LAKE

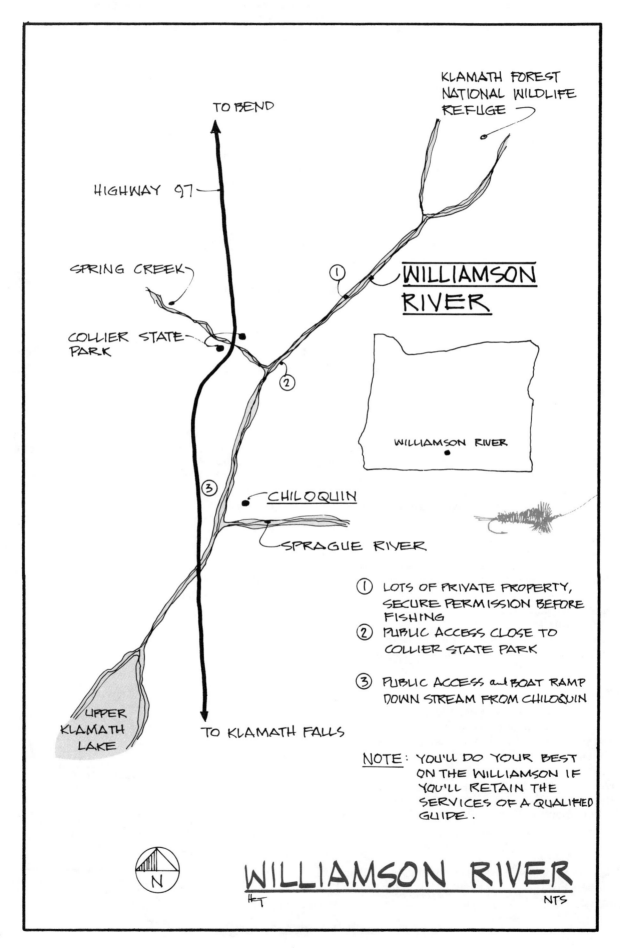

KLAMATH FOREST
NATIONAL WILDLIFE
REFUGE

TO BEND

HIGHWAY 97

SPRING CREEK

COLLIER STATE
PARK

① WILLIAMSON
RIVER

②

③

WILLIAMSON RIVER

CHILOQUIN

SPRAGUE RIVER

UPPER
KLAMATH
LAKE

TO KLAMATH FALLS

① LOTS OF PRIVATE PROPERTY,
SECURE PERMISSION BEFORE
FISHING

② PUBLIC ACCESS CLOSE TO
COLLIER STATE PARK

③ PUBLIC ACCESS and BOAT RAMP
DOWN STREAM FROM CHILOQUIN

NOTE: YOU'LL DO YOUR BEST
ON THE WILLIAMSON IF
YOU'LL RETAIN THE
SERVICES OF A QUALIFIED
GUIDE.

N

WILLIAMSON RIVER

NTS

Williamson River

A conversation I had one day with Polly Rosborough, the late and revered fly-tier, sportsman and pioneer of the Klamath County Fly Casters told me a lot about this river in a few words. He told me the Williamson is the best, "big-fish" water in the country, and I think he was right. The Williamson was one of the first rivers in Oregon to be managed for wild trout.

The Lower Williamson River, the primary fly fishing section, is located 25 miles north of Klamath Falls. It's crossed by Highway 97 near the town of Chiloquin where the Sprague River enters the Williamson. It's a big, winding river that runs through lots of private, forest and cattle land.

Fish the Williamson with large flies. Cast a little upstream, let the fly sink and swing and strip it back. In the summer, fish dries on the surface when the caddis and mayflies hatch. Many fish the October caddis hatch in the fall.

The big 3 year and older rainbows are not easy to catch. On any given day, however, you'll see more fish in the 5 to 10 lb. range splashing around on the surface than you can reasonably imagine. If you want a chance to take big trout, hire a guide and head for the Williamson. If you aren't taking a guide, the Williamson can be tough to learn, especially without a boat. Some of the spots on the accompanying map will help.

Type of Fish
Large rainbow and protected Lost River Suckers.

Equipment to Use
Rods: 4 to 7 weight, 8 1/2' - 9 1/2'.
Line: Floating and sink tip to match rod weight. Some guides like intermediate sink lines.
Leaders: Nymphs & streamers, 3x and 4x, 9' - 15'. Dry flies, 4x to 6x, 9' - 15'.
Reels: Mechanical and palm drag.
Wading: Neoprene waders, felt-soled boots, wading staff.

Flies to Use
Heavy mayfly and caddis hatches June - July.
Dry patterns: Elk Hair Caddis, Comparadun, Adams, Humpy, Irresistible, Pale Morning Dun, X Caddis, Trico, Blue Winged Olive, Hexagenia, Grasshopper and other terrestrials.
Nymphs & streamers: Pheasant Tail, Hare's Ear, Marabou Leech, Matuka, Woolly Bugger, Muddler Minnow, Zonker.

When to Fish
June through October, when the big fish move up from Upper Klamath Lake. A guide suggests time of day isn't as important as putting the fly in the right place.

Season & Limits
Late May through October. There are varying regulations on the Williamson, I suggest checking the ODFW synopsis or at a fly shop before fishing.

Accommodations & Services
Good camping facilities at Spring Creek and Williamson River. Motel, restaurants and a service station near Chiloquin, an RV park off Highway 97.

Harry's Opinion
If you haven't fished for the Williamson's big trout before, you'll save a lot of learning time and effort by hiring a qualified guide.

Rating
The Williamson is an 8 for big fish opportunity.

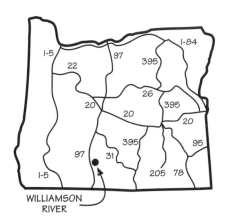

WILLIAMSON RIVER

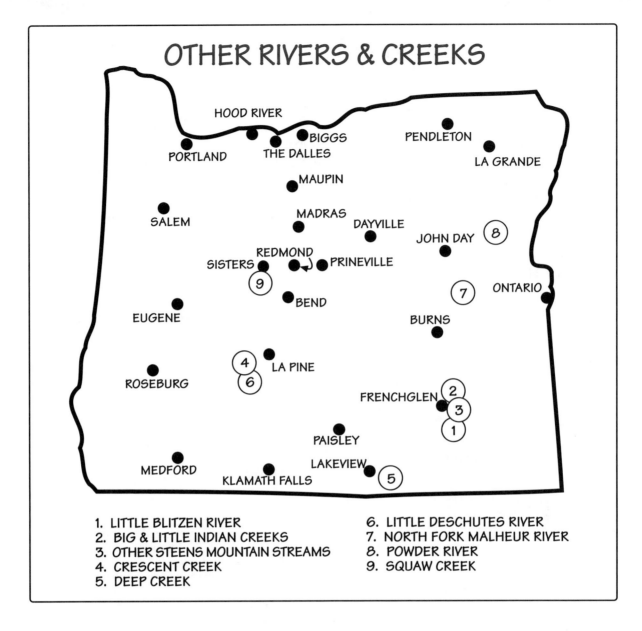

OTHER RIVERS & CREEKS

HOOD RIVER

PORTLAND   THE DALLES   BIGGS

PENDLETON

LA GRANDE

MAUPIN

SALEM

MADRAS

DAYVILLE

JOHN DAY   ⑧

REDMOND

SISTERS   PRINEVILLE

⑨

⑦   ONTARIO

BEND

EUGENE

BURNS

④   LA PINE

ROSEBURG   ⑥

② FRENCHGLEN

③

①

PAISLEY

MEDFORD   KLAMATH FALLS   LAKEVIEW   ⑤

1. LITTLE BLITZEN RIVER
2. BIG & LITTLE INDIAN CREEKS
3. OTHER STEENS MOUNTAIN STREAMS
4. CRESCENT CREEK
5. DEEP CREEK

6. LITTLE DESCHUTES RIVER
7. NORTH FORK MALHEUR RIVER
8. POWDER RIVER
9. SQUAW CREEK

*H*ere's about all you'll need to fly fish these "other" rivers and streams. Check with one of the fly shops listed in the back of this guidebook to get additional information about tackle, hatches and current conditions.

Type of Fish
Rainbow, brown, brook, bull trout.

Known Hatches
Mayflies, damselflies, caddis and midges.

Equipment to Use
Rods: 4 to 6 weight.
Line: Floating, intermediate sink to type IV's.
Leaders: 6' to 12', 3x - 4x.
Reels: Standard trout reels are fine.
Wading: Most waters are wadable with hip boots or chest-high waders.

Flies to Use
Dries: Midges, Callibaetis, Elk Hair Caddis, Adams, humpy, PMD, BWO, Renegade, Royal Wulff.

Nymphs: Scuds, Midge Pupa, Hare's Ear, Pheasant Tail, Bird's Nest, Prince, Zug Bug, Brassie, Golden Stone.
Streamers: Woolly Bugger, Zonker, Matuka, leech, Muddlers.

When to Fish
Consult a fly shop and the ODFW synopsis for the best times to fly fish.

Accommodations & Services
Some, variable or none! Ask.

Rating
When conditions are good, all are 5 or better.

Comments On Other Rivers & Creeks

Little Blitzen (1)
The Little Blitzen is a tributary of the Blitzen (Donner und Blitzen) and flows into the Blitzen about three miles down from Blitzen Crossing. Blitzen Crossing is located on the Steens Mountain Loop Road. The Little Blitzen can be accessed through the Clemens Ranch, which has been deeded to the BLM. For specific information, consult BLM personnel at their office on Highway 20 just west of Hines. The Little Blitzen is fly fishing only and catch and release.

Big Indian and Little Indian Creeks (2)
These two creeks are on the west side of the Steens Mountain and can be accessed off the Steens Mountain Loop Road. These are small creeks and they hold a good population of native rainbows. They can't stand much pressure, so please practice catch and release when you fish the creeks. Plan on doing lots of walking. The terrain along these creeks will amaze you. It's really something else.

Other Streams in the Steens Mountains (3)
You'll find numerous small streams cascading down the Steens Mountain. Names like Kiger Creek, McCoy Creek, Ankle Creek, Wild Horse Creek and Skull Creek all hold wild fish. To access some of these, you must cross private land, and that can pose a problem. Contact the BLM staff (on Highway 20 west of Hines) for some guidance.

Crescent Creek (4)
It's hardly a household word in Central Oregon, but Crescent is a nice little fly fishing water. The creek has plenty of access and a good population of brown and rainbow trout. Fly shops in Bend or the ODFW office should be able to assist you with information on Crescent Creek. Crescent Creek can be accessed off Highway 58 west of Highway 97.

Deep Creek (5)
Deep Creek is located southeast of Lakeview, Oregon and parallels Highway 140. This is a good fly fishing stream with stocked and wild fish. Check with the ODFW regional office in Hines, Oregon for more information and current conditions.

Little Deschutes River (6)
This meandering stream crosses Highway 58 east of where Crescent Creek crosses the highway. It has some good-sized brown trout and rainbows and is fairly easy to wade. If you are in a mood for exploring new trout water, you just might give the Little Deschutes a try.

North Fork of the Malheur River (7)
The section above Beulah Reservoir, that is accessible only by foot, can provide some exceptional rainbow fishing. Study a good topographical map and select a likely spot. It's my guess you'll be glad you gave the North Fork a try.

Powder River (8)
The Powder is west of Baker City and is accessed by Highway 30. The best fishing is in the tail waters of Mason and Theif Valley Dams. Rainbows run from 9 to 14 inches with an occasional fish to 18".

Squaw Creek (9)
If you're in the Sisters area and just want to poke around with a light fly rod, try Squaw Creek. This little creek comes into town from the Cascades and eventually empties into the Deschutes River above Lake Billy Chinook. Most of the fish are wild Rainbows. Ten inches is as big as you'll get. Occasionally a big one escapes a farm ponds and gets in the creek. Fish with dries like a Madam X, Renegade and Royal Wulff. Also throw in some Comparaduns, Elk Hair Caddis and a Griffith's Gnat. For nymphs, use a Brassie, Beadhead Pheasant Tail, Soft Hackle or Hare's Ear in small sizes. In the summer, forget waders and hop along the rocks. The rest of the year consider hip waders. Since these fish are wild, we strongly encourage catch and release.

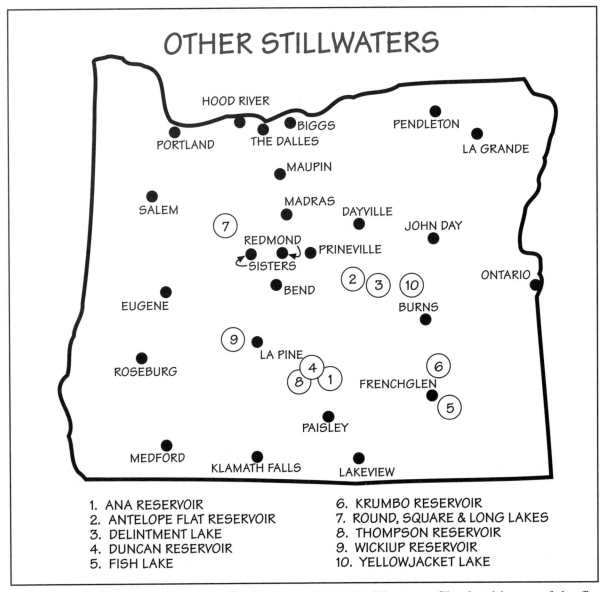

OTHER STILLWATERS

HOOD RIVER
PENDLETON
BIGGS
LA GRANDE
PORTLAND
THE DALLES
MAUPIN
SALEM
MADRAS
DAYVILLE
JOHN DAY
⑦
REDMOND
PRINEVILLE
SISTERS
ONTARIO
② ③ ⑩
BEND
BURNS
EUGENE
⑨
LA PINE
⑥
ROSEBURG
④
⑧ ①
FRENCHGLEN
PAISLEY
⑤
MEDFORD
KLAMATH FALLS
LAKEVIEW

1. ANA RESERVOIR
2. ANTELOPE FLAT RESERVOIR
3. DELINTMENT LAKE
4. DUNCAN RESERVOIR
5. FISH LAKE

6. KRUMBO RESERVOIR
7. ROUND, SQUARE & LONG LAKES
8. THOMPSON RESERVOIR
9. WICKIUP RESERVOIR
10. YELLOWJACKET LAKE

*H*ere's about all you'll need to fly fish these "other" stillwaters. Check with one of the fly shops listed in the back of this guidebook to get additional information about tackle, hatches and current conditions.

Type of Fish
Rainbow, brown, brook, bass and bluegill.

Known Hatches
Mayflies, damselflies, caddis and midges.

Equipment to Use
Rods: 4 to 7 weight.
Line: Floating, full-sink intermediate to type IV's.
Leaders: 6' to 15', 3x - 6x.
Reels: Standard trout reels are fine.
Wading: Most waters have wadable shorelines. Take a float tube if you prefer.

Flies to Use
Dries: Damsels, midges, Callibaetis, Elk Hair Caddis, Timberline Emerger, Griffith's Gnat, Comparadun, Light Cahill.

Nymphs: Scuds, damsel, dragonfly, midge, snail, Gold Ribbed Hare's Ear, Pheasant Tail, Bird's Nest, Prince, Zug Bug, Tied Down Caddis, Waterboatman.
Streamers: Woolly Bugger, Zonker, Matuka, leech.

When to Fish
Consult a fly shop and the ODFW synopsis for the best times to fish.

Accommodations & Services
Some, variable or none! Ask.

Rating
When conditions are good, all are 5 or better.

Comments On Other Stillwaters

Ana Reservoir (1)
As the source of the Ana River, this small reservoir is ice free most of the year. It's fed by springs with water temperatures of around 56 degrees. I've had some good days fly fishing here during January and February. The reservoir is stocked with rainbow trout and has a population of hybrid bass. Not a bad place to go to shrug off the winter fishing blahs.

Antelope Flat Reservoir (2)
A fair sized reservoir of about 170 acres when full. The reservoir is southeast of Prineville. Take the road from Prineville to Paulina and turn to the south onto FS #17, some 8 miles east of Post. It's roughly 11 miles to the reservoir. There are campgrounds and a boat launch at the reservoir.

Delintment Lake (3)
Delintment is about 50 acres and lies northwest of Burns. For the best access, check with BLM, ODFW or at B&B Sporting Goods. All are located in the Burns/Hines area on Highway 20. Rainbows are of good size and it's not unusual to get a fish in the 3 pound class. Most fish are 9 to 14". There's a good campground at the lake.

Duncan Reservoir (4)
This desert reservoir is near Silver Lake, east of the town of Silver Lake about 50 miles east of La Pine on Highway 31. It's had its ups and downs. If there was space, I'd relate a call I got from Cal Jordan (one of the fine fly fishers and gentlemen with whom I've had the privilege of fishing) about meeting him to fish Duncan Reservoir. In short, he'd had the best fly fishing he'd ever experienced in Oregon one day at Duncan. We went the next day, and between us, didn't have a strike. As I said, Duncan is a good fly fishery, but has its ups and downs.

Fish Lake (5)
The lake is located on the Steens Mountain and has plenty of spunky rainbows. Fly fishing can be good from the time you can access the lake (generally late June) until late October. If you go in July, load your rig with mosquito repellent. The fall period can be beautiful and you can have the lake nearly to yourself.

Krumbo Reservoir (6)
When you're in the vicinity of Frenchglen, you might want to check Krumbo Reservoir. It has a mixed bag of fish (rainbow, bass, etc.), but the rainbows get to be fairly good sized. It has a surface area of about 150 acres. You can reach Krumbo going south from Burns on Highway 205 toward Frenchglen. It will be on your left about 20 miles from the Malheur Refuge headquarters turn-off. A dirt road leads to the reservoir. It's about 4 miles from Highway 205 to the reservoir. There is food, gas, lodging and camping in and near Frenchglen.

Round, Square and Long Lakes (7)
These lakes, near the Santiam Pass can be accessed by going to Round Lake on Forest Road 1210. You'll have to walk to Square and Long Lakes. You'll find rainbow, cutthroat and brook trout in these lakes. The fish are not large, but can be fun. If you want to take the family on a nice outing, this would be a good choice. There is a primitive campground at Round Lake.

Thompson Reservoir (8)
Like Chickahominy, Thompson was hit hard by drought but has come back. This is one of the better "other" reservoirs for fly fishing. The rainbows here grow rapidly and fish in the 20" range are common. It's best to fish from a boat. Try the finger-like bays. There are good campgrounds and boat launching facilities. Thompson is about 15 miles south of the community of Silver Lake. Take Highway 31 from La Pine and turn on road 27 or Silver Creek Marsh road.

Wickiup Reservoir (9)
This is a large reservoir and has a good population of brown trout. Some are truly giants. Most people think of Wickiup as a hardware fishery, but if you take the time to learn the reservoir, Wickiup can produce excellent results for the fly fisher. Get to Wickiup from Sunriver off Road #42.

Yellowjacket Lake (10)
A small lake about 40 miles northwest of Burns. It has some nice fish and is stocked annually. It can be fished from the shore, but a float tube is a good idea. There's a good campground at the lake.

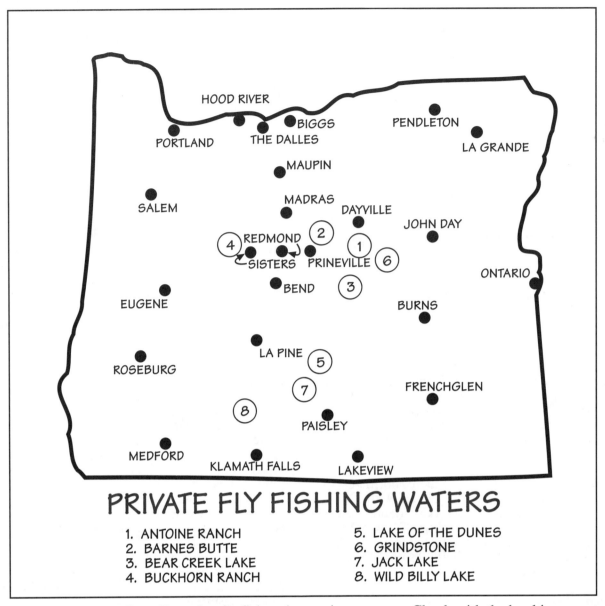

PRIVATE FLY FISHING WATERS

1. ANTOINE RANCH
2. BARNES BUTTE
3. BEAR CREEK LAKE
4. BUCKHORN RANCH
5. LAKE OF THE DUNES
6. GRINDSTONE
7. JACK LAKE
8. WILD BILLY LAKE

*H*ere's about all you'll need to fly fish at these private waters. Check with the booking agent to get additional information about tackle, hatches and any food or gear you may need.

Type of Fish
Rainbow, brown, brook, bass and bluegill.

Known Hatches
Mayflies, damselflies, caddis and midges.

Equipment to Use
Rods: 4 to 7 weight.
Line: Floating, full-sink intermediate to type IV's.
Leaders: 6' to 15', 3x - 6x.
Reels: Standard trout reels are fine.
Wading: Most of these waters have wadable shorelines. Take a float tube if that's your preferred method of fishing stillwaters.

Flies to Use
Dries: Adult damsel, suspended midge, Callibaetis parachute & spinner, Elk Hair & Slow Water Caddis, Timberline Emerger, Griffith's Gnat, Palomino, Century Drive Midge, Comparadun, Light Cahill.

Nymphs: Scud, damsel, dragonfly, midge, snail, Gold Ribbed Hare's Ear, Pheasant Tail, Bird's Nest, Soft Hackle, Prince, Zug Bug, Tied Down Caddis, Carey Special, Cates Turkey, Waterboatman.
Streamers: Woolly Buggers, Zonker, Matuka, leech patterns.

When to Fish
Consult the booking agents for the private "season" and the best times to fish.

Accommodations & Services
Some, variable or none! Ask.

Rating
When conditions are good, all are 8 or better.

Private Fly Fishing Waters

*T*he Central Oregon region has excellent options to fly fishing public waters. Often "pay" fly fishing is the only way to achieve seclusion and reliable fly fishing. Because you paid money, however, you're not assured of landing fish. You'll still need to apply considerable skill and thought to catch fish from these waters. Also, these waters have been in operation for a number of years and each is unique and worth the money. Call the contact numbers in advance for reservations, information and conditions.

Antoine Ranch (1)   This ranch is known throughout the Northwest for excellent fishing. Located 65 miles east of Prineville, the ranch has 40,000 acres of private timber covered slopes, steep draws and grass covered plateaus. Angler numbers are limited weekly. Anglers can access six lakes offering trophy rainbow trout. Day fishing and guided fishing packages available. Cabins and meals included. *Contact:* Shawn at Go West Outfitters (541) 447-4082.

Barnes Butte (2)   Just outside the city of Prineville, Barnes offers bass, bluegill and Kamloops trout. Mixing different techniques for the varied species can be fun (The Barnes Butte Grand Slam). Trout fishing is good all year. Bass and bluegill are more active in warm weather months. Float tubing is popular, but a small boat (with an electric motor) is also a good way to fish. *Contacts:* Roger Hudspeth (541) 447-4400, The Fly Box (541) 388-3330, The Fly Fisher's Place, (541) 549-3474.

Bear Creek Lake (3)   This 35 acre lake, about 60 miles east of Bend, is fairly new but receives rave reviews. The lake is rich in aquatic life, especially damselflies and dragonflies. Also bring Water Boatman, leeches, snails, scuds and midges. Rainbows average 16" to 18", but be prepared for the big tug from 5-7 pounders. Fishing is best from mid-April through early summer and late fall. At 4,600' cool water keeps fishing consistent. Day trips available for 2 to 6 anglers or rent a cabin for groups staying overnight. *Contact:* The Fly Box (541) 388-3330.

Buckhorn Ranch (4)   About 20 minutes east of Sisters, this 15 acre lake offers one of the best and nearby opportunities to catch & release BIG Kamloops and Rainbow trout. The lake is full of damselflies, dragonflies and caddis and is surrounded by hundreds of acres of farm and pasture land. There is plenty cover and rock outcroppings. Casting from the bank is easy but a float tube is the best way to fish Buckhorn. Fish from March - July and again from September - December. Day trips only: *Contact:* Marc Thalacker (541) 923-6227.

Lake of the Dunes (5)   Located near Summer Lake, about 75 miles southeast of La Pine, these 4 lakes range in size from 4 to 6 acres. All hold trophy rainbow trout that will test your skills. Two large artesian wells feed the lakes with cold water. Callibaetis hatches are strong, and dry fly fishing is good most of the season. Prepare for other hatches and don't forget slow sinking lines for fishing nymphs and leeches. Concentrate on sneaky approaches from the bank. Hip boots are ideal. A rustic log cabin on site sleeps 5 and rents for overnight stays. Fly fishing only, March 1 to October 31. This is one of the better fly fishing bargains east of the Cascades. *Contacts:* The Fly Fisher's Place (541) 549-3474, The Patient Angler (541) 389-6208.

Grindstone (6)   East of the town of Paulina, this ranch is in a magnificent high desert setting. Four lakes, rich with scuds, leeches and snails, hold trophy rainbow trout. Trout get "shoulders" here and fight hard. Dry fly fishing can be outrageous at times. Multiday packages include lodging and food. Bring a float tube to access the best fishing. Guides can show you the waters and help with techniques. *Contact:* Bill Beardsley (541) 330-5508.

Jack Lake (7)   This 27 acre lake is adjacent to giant Summer Lake, about 85 miles south and east of La Pine. This perfect spot for float tubing sports a very convenient access ramp. Plenty of huge 20 - 28" Donaldson and Redside trout are available. Trout Unlimited members can purchase annual fishing privileges ($500). A portion benefits Oregon T.U. habitat projects. The fishery is managed by enterprising Darrell Seven who operates Summer Lake Inn, about 9 miles from the lake. The Inn has cabins and rooms, all with views. Good fishing is available at the 3 acre pond which runs alongside the cabins. *Contacts:* Darrell Seven (800) 261-2778, www.summerlakeinn.com, Fly Fisher's Place (541) 549-3474.

Wild Billy Lake (8)   A beautiful 200 acre lake in south central Oregon. Fly fishing only for big Kamloops and Mt. Lassen rainbows and Donaldson Steelhead (to 14 lbs.). Float tubing is the most popular way to fish. Small boats (no gas motors) are allowed. Picnic and camp sites at the lake with a cabin planned for 1999. A motel and restaurant are within driving distance. *Contacts:* Ron Thienes (541)747-5595, Sunriver Fly Shop (541)593-8814.

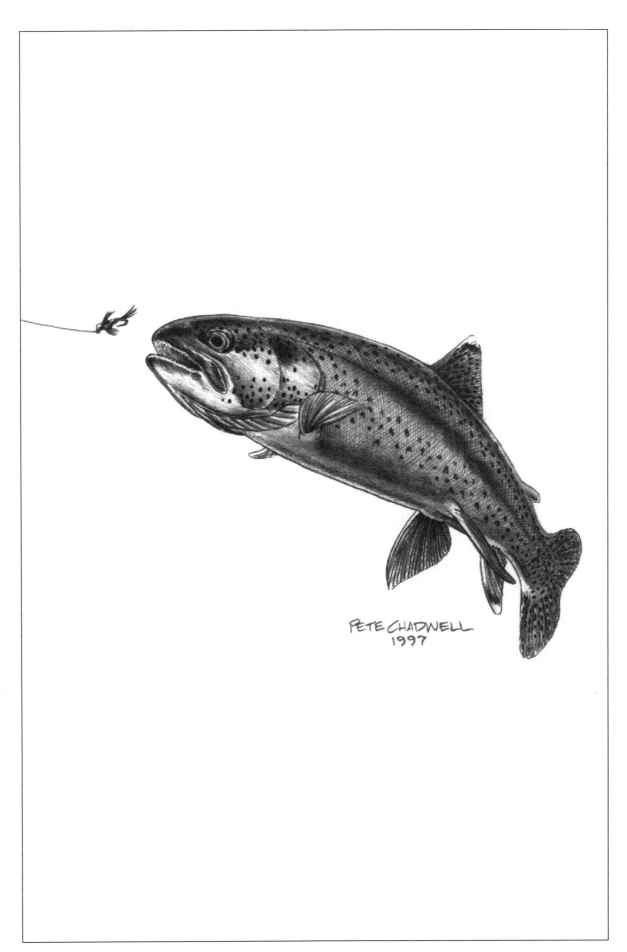

Rainbow Trout

Appendix

Oregon Fly Tackle

Western Oregon

The Caddis Fly
Angling Shop
168 W Sixth Street
Eugene OR 97401
(541) 342-7005

CountrySport
126 SW First Ave.
Portland, OR 97204
(503) 221-4545

Creekside Fly Shop
346 High Street South
Salem, OR 97301
(503) 588-1768

Fly Country Outfiters
3400 State Street, #6704
South Salem, OR 97301
(503) 585-4898

The Fly Fishing Shop
68248 E. Hwy 26
Hoodland Park Plaza
Welches, OR 97067
(503) 622-4607

Home Waters Fly Fishing
444 West Third Ave.
Eugene, OR 97401
(541) 342-6691

Kaufmann's Streamborn
8861 SW Commercial
Tigard, OR 97223
(503) 639-6400

The Scarlet Ibis
6905 NW Kings Blvd.
Corvallis, OR 97330
(541) 754-1544

Central Oregon

Camp Sherman Store
25451 Forest Service Rd.
Camp Sherman, OR 97730
(541) 595-6711

Deschutes Canyon Fly Shop
7 N Highway 197
Maupin, OR 97037
(541) 395-2565

Deschutes River Outfitters
61115 S. Highway 97
Bend, OR 97701
(541) 388-8191

The Fly Box
923 SE Third Street
Bend, OR 97701
(541) 388-3330

The Fly Fisher's Place
151 West Main St.
Sisters, OR 97759
(541) 549-3474

The Hook
Bldg 21, Sunriver Mall
Sunriver, OR 97707
(541) 593-2358

The Oasis
Hwy 197 S.
Maupin, OR 97037
(541) 395-2611

Oscar's Sporting Goods
380 SW 15th Street
Madras, OR 97741
(541) 475-2962

The Patient Angler
55 NW Wall Street
Bend, OR 97701
(541) 389-6208

Prineville Sporting Goods
346 N. Deer St.
Prineville, OR 97754
(541) 447-6883

Sunriver Fly Shop
Sunriver Business Park
Sunriver, OR 97707
(541) 593-8814

Williamson River Anglers
Junction Hwy 97& Hwy 62
Chiloquin, OR 97624
(541) 783-2677

Eastern Oregon

B & B Sporting Goods
Highway 20 & W. Conley,
Hines, OR 97738
(541) 573-6200

Other Helpful Fly Shops

Reno Fly Shop
294 E. Moana Lane #14
Reno, NV 89502
(702) 825-3474

The Fly Shop
4140 Churn Creek Rd.
Redding, CA 96002
1 (800) 669-3474

Bill Mason Sun Valley
Outfitters
Sun Valley Mall
Sun Valley, ID 83353
(208) 622-9305

Clubs & Associations

Oregon Council
Federation of Fly Fishers
987 Travis Street
Eugene, OR 97404

Angler's Club of Portland
PO Box 9235
Portland, OR 97207

Cascade Family Fly Fishers
PO Box 70453
Eugene, OR 97709

Central Oregon Fly Fishers
PO Box 1126
Bend, OR 97709

Clackamas Fly Fishers
PO Box 268
West Linn, OR 97068

Columbia Gorge Fly Fishers
1027 Verdant St. West
The Dalles, OR 97058
Klamath County Fly Casters
PO Box 324
Klamath Falls, OR 97601

Lower Umpqua Fly Fishers
PO Box 521
Reedsport, OR 97467

McKenzie Fly Fishers
PO Box 10865
Eugene, OR 97440-2865

Mid-Willamette Fly
Fishers
PO Box 22
Corvallis, OR 97339

Northwest Fly Fishers
PO Box 656
Troutdale, OR 97060

Rainland Flycasters
PO Box 1045
Astoria, OR 97103

Rogue Fly Fishers
PO Box 4637
Medford, OR 97501

Santiam Fly Casters, Inc.
PO Box 691
Salem, OR 97308

Silver Fox Flycasters
802 Schlador St.
Silverton, OR 97381

The Steamboaters
233 Howard Ave.
Eugene, OR 97404

Sunriver Anglers
PO Box 4237
Sunriver, OR 97707

California Trout
870 Market Street
Suite #859
San Francisco, CA 94102
(415) 392-8887

The Federation
of Fly Fishers
National Headquarters
1(800) 618-0808
Call for local club
www.wsa.com/ool

International Game
Fish Association
(305) 467-0161
3000 E. Las Olas Blvd.
Fort Lauderdale, FL 33316

National Fresh Water
Fishing Hall of Fame
(715) 634-4440
P.O. Box 33
Hayward, WI 54843

Additional Information

Government Resources, Oregon

Oregon Department of Fish and Wildlife (ODFW) Headquarters
2501 SW First St.
Portland, OR 97207
(503) 229-5400

ODFW Central
61374 Parrell Rd.
Bend, OR 97702
(541) 388-6363

ODFW Southast
237 S. Hines Blvd.
PO Box 8

ODFW The Dalles
(541) 296-4628

Hines, OR 97738
(541) 573-6582

ODFW John Day
(541) 575-1167

ODFW Klamath Falls
(541) 883-5732

ODFW Lakeview
(541) 947-2950

ODFW Madras
(541) 475-2183

ODFW Ontario
(541) 889-6975

ODFW Prineville
(541) 447-5111

Bureau of Land Management
Oregon State Office
PO Box 2965
Portland, OR 97208
(503) 231-6281

BLM Map Distribution Unit
Rm 17, State Hwy Bldg.
Salem, OR 97310
(503) 378-6254

Burns District
Highway 20
Hines, OR

US and Oregon Forest Service Offices

US Forest Service
PO Box 3623
Portland, OR 97208

Deschutes Natl. Forest
(541) 388-5664

Malheur Natl. Forest
(541) 575-1731

Ochoco Natl. Forest
(541) 477-6247

Winema Natl. Forest
(541) 883-6714

Oregon State Forestry
2600 State St.
Salem, OR 97310
(503) 378-2504

Oregon State Parks
Camping (503) 238-7488

Oregon Dept. Of Forestry
Maps (541) 378-2504

Oregon Dept. Of Transportation
(541) 378-6254

Oregon Dept. Of Tourism
(541) 378-3451

Warm Springs
Indian Reservation
(541) 378-3671

References and Other Reading Material

Oregon Sport Fishing Regulations
Oregon Department of Fish and Wildlife

Oregon Atlas and Gazetteer
Delorme Mapping

Fishing In Oregon
Casali and Diness

Fishing Oregon's Deschutes River
Scott Richmond

Hatch Guide for Western Streams
Jim Schollmeyer

Hatch Guide for Western Lakes
Jim Schollmeyer

Mayflies
Malcolm Knopp &
Robert Cornier

Caddisflies
Gary Lafontaine

Western Hatches
Rick Hafele &
Dave Huges

Fly Fishing The Internet
www.fedflyfishers.org
www.flyshop.com
www.flyfishamerica.com
www. gofishing.com
www.ffa.com
www.fly-fishing-women.com
www.tu.org/troutor/m/metolrec/htm
www.flyfishing.com.asf
www.ool.com/fff
www.ohwy.com
www.amrivers.org
www.gorp.com
www.flyfishto.com

Guidebooks
www.amazon.com
www.bookzone.com
www.powells.com
www.booksnow.com
www.justgoodbooks.com
www.adventurous traveloer.com
barnesandnoble.com

Air Travel
American
www. americanair.com
Alaskan
www. alaskaair.com
Continental
www. flycontinental.com
Delta
www. delta-air.com
Northwest
www. nwa.com
Southwest
www. southwest.com
Trans World
www. southwest.com
United
www. ual.com
USAirways
www. usair.com
Travel Agent
www.itn.com
www.thetrip.com
www.travelweb.com
www.previewtravel.com

Central Oregon Hatches

By Jeff Perin

	J	F	M	A	M	J	J	A	S	O	N	D	
Blue Wing Olive (*Baetis* Sp.)	X	X	X	X	X	X	X	X	X	X		X	All rivers, very prolific, important.
March Brown (*Rhithrogena* Sp.)			X	X	X								Especially important on McKenzie & Deschutes.
Pale Morning Dun (*Epemerella* Sp.)				X	X	X	X	X	X	X			Very important on all rivers & spring creeks.
Callibaetis				X	X	X	X	X	X	X			Super stillwater hatch. ①
Mahogany Dun (*Nixe* Sp. also *Paraleptophlebia* Sp.)						X	X	X	X	X			Strong hatches on Deschutes, Fall, Metolius & Crooked.
Hexagenia							X	X	X	X			Important on Williamson.
Pale Evening Dun (*Heptagenia* Sp.)				X	X	X	X	X	X	X			Strong on Deschutes, hatches on fast moving rivers.
Cinygmula also *Cinygma* Sp.			X	X	X		X	X	X				Great early & late season hatch on Metolius.
Trico						X	X	X	X	X			Good hatches on Ana & Williamson.
Western Green Drake (*Drunella* Sp.)					X	X	X		X	X			Metolius "SuperHatch" also Fall River, McKenzie & Deschutes
Terrestrials					X	X	X	X	X	X			Ants & Hoppers productive. Also beetle.
Salmon Fly					X	X							The Big One. Hit right, one of best on the Deschutes.
Special Metolius hatches							X	X	X	X			
Goldenstone					X	X	X						Prolific on Deschutes, unbelievable hatches on Metolius.
Special Metolius hatches							X	X	X	X			

① Note that locally important hatches of Grey Drakes (Siphlonurus), Caenis and Centroptilum may provide good fishing at times.

X= Prime Hatch
X= Other possible hatch times producing localized light to heavy activity.

Central Oregon Hatches

By Jeff Perin

	J	F	M	A	M	J	J	A	S	O	N	D	
Little Olive Stone								X	X	X			Late afternoons & evenings, espcially Metolius.
Yellow Sally							X	X	X				Cold rivers on warm days for this beautiful hatch.
Little Black Stone	X	X	X										Early season if water conditions good.
Longhorned Sedge *(Oecetis)*					X	X	X	X	X				Great caddis hatch on lakes, especially edges.
Traveling Caddis					X	X	X	X	X				Most common big caddis hatching in high lakes, warm evenings.
Green Sedge *(Rhyacophila)*					X	X	X	X	X	X	X		Caddis important in all 3 stages. Larva is commonly called Green Rock Worm.
Spotted Sedge *(Hydropsyche)*				X	X	X	X	X	X	X	X		Both the pupa & adult are very important especially in the large to mid-size streams
October Caddis *(Dicosmoecus & Neophylax)*								X	X	X		X	Large caddis, usually pupa works best. Sometimes use for Bull trout & Steelhead.
Silver Stripe Sedge *(Hesperophylax)*	X	X	X						X	X	X	X	Hatches odd times of year. Usually pupa produces best.
Various Micro-caddis			X	X	X	X	X	X	X	X	X		Fish gorge on #18 to #24 black or brown caddis. Try CDC caddis to match hatch.

Central Oregon Hatches

By Jeff Perin

	J	F	M	A	M	J	J	A	S	O	N	D	
American Grannom (*Brachycentrus Sp.*)			X	X	X	X	X	X	X				Amazing hatch many years. Trout may feed on larva before hatch. Pupa & egg laying adults most active.
Little Western Weedy Water Sedge (*Amiocentrus*)					X	X	X	X	X				Try cased caddis or small green pupa, dead drift in riffles or weed beds.
Saddle Case Maker/ Little Tan Short-Horn Sedge (*Glossosoma*)				X	X	X	X	X	X				Small cream larva is good in the riffles. Pupas good evening, especially spring.
Tube Case Maker/ Speckled Peter (*Helicopsyche*)					X	X	X	X					Good spring creek hatch, also found in slower sections of rivers. Use yellow pupa or adult.
Little Sister Sedge (*Cheumato-psyche*)				X	X	X	X	X	X				Wide distribution, prolific. One of the most important of all the caddis. Fish all 3 stages.
Brown Sedge (*Lepidostoma*)						X	X	X					Try a brown Elk Hair Caddis, a great searching pattern for this hatch.
Little Western Dark Sedge (*Oligophebodes*)					X	X	X	X					This small caddis makes itself important in all stages of the life cycle. A spent egg layer is the most fun to fish.
Black Dancers (*Mystacides*)						X	X	X	X				Especially important along the margins of lakes.

Central Oregon Hatches

By Jeff Perin

	J	F	M	A	M	J	J	A	S	O	N	D	
Pale Western Stream Sedge *(Chyranda)*						X	X	X	X	X			Good evening hatch. Try running a yellow pupa behind an adult about 20".
Damselfly					X	X	X	X					Nymphs are most important but when trout feed on the adults it's pure chaos!
Dragonfly					X	X	X	X					Nymphs are most important.
Water-boatman			X	X	X	X	X	X	X	X			Mostly in lakes.
Scud	X	X	X	X	X	X	X	X	X	X	X	X	Lots of trout get fat on scuds, fish them in lakes & rivers.
Midges *(Chironomidae)*	X	X	X	X	X	X	X	X	X	X	X	X	Little 2 winged insects very important on all Oregon rivers, & lakes.

Weigh Your Catch With a Tape Measure

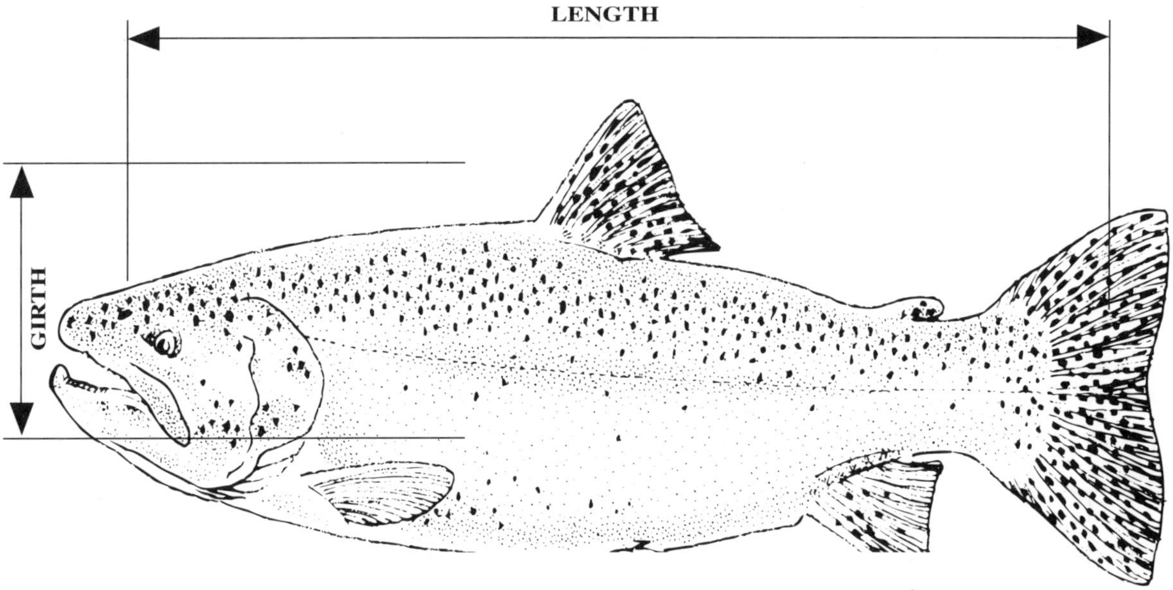

EXAMPLE: A fish 20" long and 14" around (at its thickest part) weighs 4.9 pounds.

Girth (inches) \ Length (inches)	10	12	14	16	18	20	22	24	26	28	30
8	0.8	1.0	1.1	1.3	1.4	1.6	1.8	1.9	2.1	2.2	2.4
10	1.3	1.5	1.8	2.0	2.3	2.5	2.8	3.0	3.3	3.5	3.8
12	1.8	2.2	2.5	2.9	3.2	3.6	4.0	4.3	4.7	5.0	5.4
14	2.5	2.9	3.4	3.9	4.4	4.9	5.4	5.9	6.4	6.9	7.4
16	3.2	3.8	4.5	5.1	5.8	6.4	7.0	7.7	8.3	9.0	9.6
18	4.1	4.9	5.7	6.5	7.3	8.1	8.9	9.7	10.5	11.3	12.2
20	5.0	6.0	7.0	8.0	9.0	10.0	11.0	12.0	13.0	14.0	15.0

Length (inches)
Tip of nose to notch at the center of tail.

Courtesy of Ralph & Lisa Cutter's California School of Flyfishing • P.O. Box 8212, Truckee, CA 96162 • 1 (800) 58-TROUT

No Nonsense Fly Fishing Knots

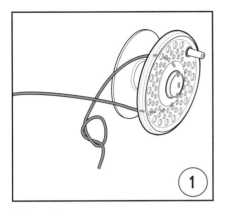 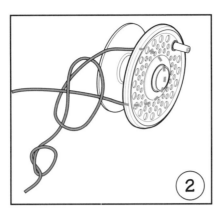 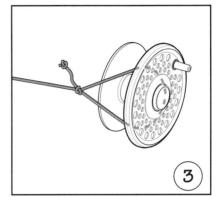

Arbor Knot Use this knot to attach backing to your fly reel. 75 yards of backing will be plenty for most of Oregon's waters.

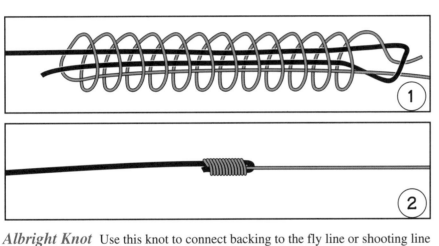

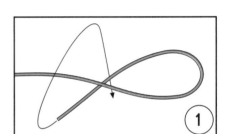

Albright Knot Use this knot to connect backing to the fly line or shooting line

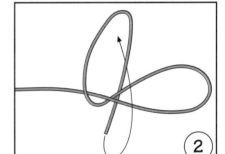

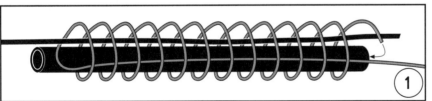

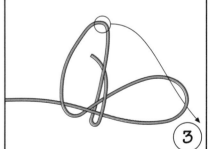

FLY LINE

LEADER

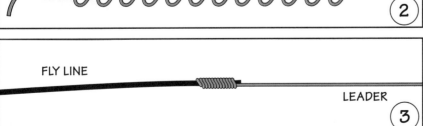

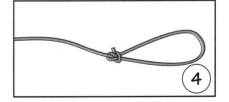

Nail Knot Use a nail, needle or a small tube to tie this knot, which connects the forward end of the fly line to the butt end of the leader. Follow this with a Prefection Loop, and you've got a permanent end loop that allows easy leader changes.

Perfection Loop Use this knot to create a loop in the butt end of the leader. You can easily "loop-to-loop" your leader to your fly line.

❖ IX ❖

No Nonsense Fly Fishing Knots

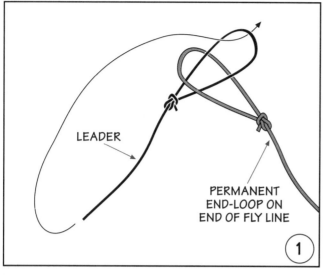

Loop To Loop Use this simple knot to connect the leader to an end loop on the tip of the fly line

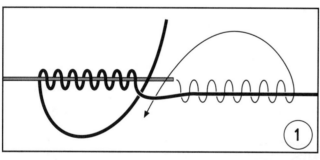

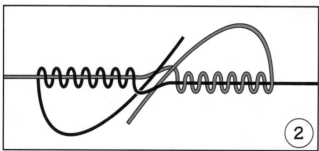

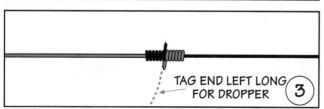

Blood Knot Use this knot to connect sections of leader material. To add a dropper, leave the heavier tag end long and attach fly.

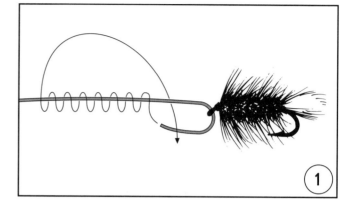

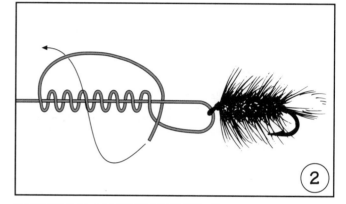

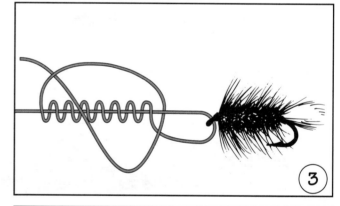

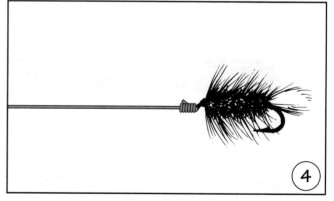

Improved Clinch Knot Use this knot to attach a fly to the end of the tippet. Remember to moisten the knot just before you pull it tight.

❖ X ❖

Fly Fishing Terms

Action adj. Used to describe the relative resistance to bending as you move down the length of a particular fly rod.

Attractor n. A fly that is designed to look like no life form in particular, but rather to just attract the attention of the quarry and give the impression of being something good to eat.

Backing n. A very strong, thin braided line tied to the fly reel and to which you attach the fly line itself.

Barbless adj. A type of hook which does not have a barb on the pointed end. Barbs were thought to assist in keeping the hook from being shaken lose by the fish. Research shows barbless hooks hold as well if tension is kept on the line by the fisher.

Beadhead adj. Describes a nymph or wetfly which has a small brass or chrome bead placed on the hook ahead of the fly pattern.

Blood Knot n. A knot used to tie tippet material to the end of a leader. A very difficult knot to tie.

Bluegill n. A small, warm-water sunfish found just about everywhere in America.

Brook Trout n. (Salvelinus fontinalis) A trout-like fish indigenous to the Northeast and Midwest United States. Not actually a trout but rather a member of the Char family.

Brown Trout n. (Salmo trutta) A trout originally indigenous to Europe, Brown Trout can now be found all over America and Canada, as well as many other countries in the world.

Caddis Fly n. (Order Trichoptera) A very common waterborne insect with wings held back and up at a 45 degree angle.

Catch and Release n. The practice of releasing all fish caught with a fly rod unharmed. It is based on a value that the fishing experience is more important than keeping fish.

Char n. (Salvelinus) American Brook Trout and Lake Trout are examples of Char found in the United States. Char are cousins of trout, and breed with them, but their offspring are sterile.

Cranefly n. The "Daddy Longlegs" of the flying insect world, they are fished mainly as terrestrials, and can be fished very effectively in late summer and early fall.

Cutthroat Trout n. (Oncorhynchus clarki) A trout originally indigenous to the Western drainages of the Rocky Mountains, it is distinguished by red throat slashes under its jaw.

Damselfly n. (Enallagma cyathigarum) A large aquatic fly characterized by a long skinny, blue thorax and wings that are held back at an angle.

Disk Drag n. A mechanical method of applying resistance to fly line as it is drawn out by a fish that is hooked.

Dolly Varden n. A Char that often runs to the sea.

Double Haul n. A type of cast characterized by the quick pulling in and releasing of line in both the backcast and the forecast.

Double Taper adj. Describes a fly line that tapers at each end, allowing the user to reverse the line when one end wears out.

Dun n. The stage of a waterborne insect just after it has emerged and has the ability to fly.

Emerger n. That stage in the development of a waterborne insect when it leaves its shuck and emerging into a flying insect.

False Cast v. The act of forecasting and backcasting without ever delivering the fly to the water.

Ferrule n. The method used to join two sections of a fly rod.

Fly Fishing n. The highest form of fishing.

Fly Line n. The thick-bodied line attached to the backing, which is used to actually cast the fly.

Fry n. A baby fish.

Grayling n. (Thymallus thymallus) An elegant looking member of the salmonid family of fish that looks like a silver colored trout (but isn't a trout) and has a very large dorsal (top) fin.

Hatch n. The time when a species of waterborne insect is emerging and becoming a flying insect.

Improved Clinch Knot n. A knot used to tie a fly to the end of a leader or to a tippet.

Keeper n. A small wire ring located just in front of the grip or handle on a fly rod.

Lake Trout n. (Salvelinus namaycush) Not real trout, they are members of the Char family. They not only live in lakes, they also spawn there.

Leader n. A thin, clear monofilament tapered line attached to the end of the fly line, to which either the tippet or fly is attached.

Loading n. The act of bending a fly rod at the end of a back cast, which is caused by the weight of the fly line transferring its weight into stored energy held in the bent fly rod.

Mayfly n. (Order Ephemeroptera) A very common waterborne insect characterized by wings held in a nearly vertical position.

Mend v. To move the fly line upstream from the fly.

Midge n. (Order Diptera) A very small, mosquito-type fly often imitated by fly tiers.

Nail Knot n. A common knot used to tie the backing to the fly line and the leader to the fly line.

Nipper n. a device used to cut line quickly and neatly.

Nymph n. An undeveloped insect. Nymphs live under the water for months prior to emerging into a winged insect.

Pack Rod n. A fly rod that breaks down into between 3 and 6 pieces, which allows it to be packed into remote areas easily.

Polarized Sun Glasses n. A vital part of the fly-fisher's outfit. Three functions: 1) They allow the fisher to see into the water past the glare from reflected light from the sun. 2) They shade eyes from harmful UV rays. 3) They protect eyes from hooks.

Pool n. A location in a stream where the water is deeper than most other locations and the water runs slower.

Popper n. A floating lure used to catch warm-water fish such as bass or bluegill.

Rainbow Trout n. (*Oncorhynchus mykiss*) A Trout which is indigenous to the Pacific drainages of the Rocky Mountains; it is known for the rich pinkish colorations along the center line of the fish.

Reach Cast n. A Cast which is used when fishing downstream or when your need extra slack in your line.

Rest the Water v. Allowing the water to clam down after some form of disturbance.

Rise v. A fish coming to the surface and feeding on some food source found there.
Roll Cast n. A cast used where there is little or no room behind the fisher for a backcast.

Run n. A location in a stream characterized by shallow running water over a rocky streambed that feeds into a pool.

Salmon n. A large member of the *salmonidae* fish family which hatch in fresh water and migrate to a lake or the ocean. Some return to the stream of their origin to spawn and then die.

Scud n. A very small cold water crustacean often erroneously referred to as "freshwater shrimp."

Sea Run adj. A term applied to trout that hatch in fresh water and then migrate to the sea to grow to adulthood, then return to their natal waters to spawn.

Shooting Line n. The act of releasing extra line held in the free hand as the line passes the caster in the forecast.

Shooting Taper adj. Used to describe a rather short (45-46 feet) fly line with a majority of the weight out at the front end.

Single Action adj. A fly reel that has fixed drag, set at the factory, that cannot be adjusted by the user.

Sink Tip adj. A floating fly line with about ten feet of sinking line built into, or attached to, the front end.

Spinner n. The final stage of a waterborne insect during the mating session, when it falls, fatigued, to the water and dies.

Spinner Fall n. That time when many thousands of waterborne insects like Mayflies and Caddis Flies fall to the water in their last mortal stage.

Spring Creek n. A stream that originates from water coming up from the ground, as opposed to a freestone stream which originates from run-off or snow melt.

Steelhead n. A type of rainbow trout that migrates from the stream or river in which it is hatched to the ocean or a large landlocked lake.

Stocker adj. Term used to describe a fish which was born and raised in a hatchery and then placed in a stream, river or lake for sport fishing purposes.

Stonefly n. (*Order Plecoptera*) A large aquatic fly that emerges by crawling out of the water onto a stone or rock and then splits its shuck and becomes a flying insect.

Streamer n. A fly that imitates a small fish, worm, leech, etc.

Strike Indicator n. A floating substance, most commonly foam or yarn, attached to the leader above a nymph or other wet fly.

Strip v. Retrieval of the fly line with the hand not holding the fly rod.

Structure n. Large objects in a stream or lake, such as big rocks, trees, dock pilings, etc., around which fish will stay.

Surgeon's Knot n. An easy knot to tie, it is used to attach tippet material to the end of a leader.

Tail Out n. A location in a stream found at the end of a pool, where it again becomes shallow, fast-moving water over a rocky or sandy bottom.

Tailwaters n. A river that's fed from the bottom of a dam.

Terrestrial n. A fly tied to imitate an insect that was not born in the water, such as a grasshopper, cricket, ant, or beetle.

Tippet Material n. Very thin, monofilament material added to the end of a leader to extend the length or to rebuild the leader after some of the tippet section has been used up tying knots or broken off in fishing.

Trout n. A member of the *salmonids* family of fish that are major targets for fly fishers.

Wader Belt n. A stretchable belt worn around the waist of a pair of waders, intended to keep the water out of waders should the wearer slip and fall into the water.

Weight n. An accepted system of measuring fly line size. Fly lines come in Weights from 1 (the lightest) to 15 (the heaviest). Not necessarily a function of line strength, it is determined by the actual weight of the first 30 feet of line.

Weight Forward adj. Used to describe a fly line designed with more weight toward the front of the fly line to assist in casting.

Wet Fly n. A fly fished below, or in the surface film of water.

Wild adj. A term applied to fish that were born in the waters in which they are found, as opposed to fish that were raised in a hatchery and stocked into their current waters.

Woolly Bugger n. A type of wet fly tied to imitate nothing in particular, but rather to give the impression of a number of underwater food items a fish may be interested in.

"X" Ratings n. A system of describing the approximate thickness of leaders and tippet material. The X system runs from 010X (equaling .021 diameter at the tippet = very large) down to 7X (equaling .004 diameter at the tippet = smaller than a human hair).

Definitions from *The Easy Field Guide to Fly-Fishing Terms & Tips* by David Phares. For the complete list of terms, tips and some humor send $2.00 to: Primer Publishers 5738 North Central Avenue Phoenix, Arizona 85012

About
No Nonsense Guides

Bill Mason
Bill Mason's No Nonsense Guide
To Fly Fishing In Idaho
The Henry's Fork, Salmon, Snake and Silver Creek plus 24 other waters.

Mr. Mason penned the first fly fishing guidebook to Idaho in 1994. It features the best fly fishing waters and showcases Bill's 30 plus years of Idaho fly fishing experience.

Bill helped build a major outfitting operation at the Henry's Fork and helped open the first fly shop in Boise. In Sun Valley he developed the first fly fishing school and guiding program at Snug Fly Fishing, a fly shop he operated for 15 years. Bill eventually purchased the shop, renaming it Bill Mason Sun Valley Outfitters which has served fly fishers for over 20 years.

Jackson Streit
Jackson Streit's No Nonsense Guide
To Fly Fishing In Colorado
The Colorado, Rio Grande, Platte, Gunnison, Mountain lakes and more.

Mr. Streit has fly fished in Colorado for over 27 years. This vast experience was condensed into the third No Nonsense fly fishing guidebook, published in 1995 and updated, improved and reprinted in 1997.

In 1971 Jackson started the first guide service in the Breckenridge area. In 1985 he opened the region's first fly shop, The Mountain Angler, which he owns and manages.

Mr. Streit has fly fished the western United States, many countries and various tropical islands. He's written numerous fly fishing articles and is involved in many Trout Unlimited activities.

Ken Hanley
Ken Hanley's No Nonsense Guide
To Fly Fishing In Northern California
The Sacramento, Hat Creek, Russian, resevoirs, saltwater and bass on a fly.

Mr. Hanley has fished all the waters in this guide. While traveling the world and leading adventure expeditions he's caught over 50 species of gamefish. He's also written much on the subject including three other books.

Ken writes outdoor related pieces for a variety of magazines and newspapers. This highly enthusiastic speaker and tier is sought by fly fishing clubs, expositions and trade shows.

Terry Barron
Terry Barron's No Nonsense Guide
To Fly Fishing Pyramid Lake
The "Gem of the Desert" is fly fishing for huge Lahontan Cutthroat trout.

In 1963, while skipping high school, Mr. Barron got his first look at Pyramid Lake and was intrigued for life. Since then he's become the Reno-area and Pyramid Lake fly fishing guru. He helped establish the Truckee River Fly Fishers Club, a fly fishing guide business and he ties flies and works for the Reno Fly Shop.

Terry has recorded, for years, the pertinent information to fly fish the most outstanding trophy cutthroat fishery in the U.S. . Where else can you get tired catching 18-25" trout? Pyramid Lake. Terry's guidebook explains how to catch (and release) Lahontan cutts this size and larger. It is the first No Nonsense guidebook devoted to one unique fishery.

Taylor Streit
Taylor Streit's No Nonsense Guide
To Fly Fishing In New Mexico
The San Juan, Cimarron, Gila, Chama, Rio Grand, mountain lakes and more.

The first all inclusive guide to the top fly fishing waters in the "Land of Enchantment". Since 1970 Mr. Streit has been *THE* New Mexico fly fishing authority and #1 professional guide. He's also developed many fly patterns used throughout the region. Taylor owned the Taos Fly Shop for ten years and managed a bone fishing lodge in the Bahamas. He makes winter fly fishing pilgrimages to Argentina where he escorts fly fishers and explores.

Dave Stanley
Dave Stanley's No Nonsense Guide
To Fly Fishing In Nevada
The Truckee, Walker, Carson, Eagle, Davis, Ruby, mountain lakes and more.

Mr. Stanley is recognized nationwide as the most knowledgeable fly fisher and outdoorsman in the state of Nevada. He also travels throughout the west and other warm climes where he leads fly fishing excursions. He own's and operates the Reno Fly Shop and a satellite shop in Truckee, California. His life of fly angling and Nevada experience combines into a must read guidebook to Nevada's secluded waters.

The guide's talented coauthor, **Jeff Cavender**, is a Nevada native and manager of the Reno Fly Shop. Jeff teaches fly casting and tying. He's taught and guided all over Nevada and California during the past 30 + years.

Where No Nonsense Guides Come From

No Nonsense guidebooks give a quick, clear, understanding of the essential information needed to fly fish a region's most outstanding waters. The authors are highly experienced and qualified local fly fishers. Maps are tidy versions of the authors sketches.

These guides are produced by the fly fishers, their friends, and spouses of fly fishers, at David Communications. The publisher is located in the tiny Western town of Sisters, Oregon, just a few miles from the Metolius River.

All who produce No Nonsense guides believe in providing top quality products at a reasonable price. We also believe all information should be verified. We never hesitate to go out, fly rod in hand, to verify the facts and figures that appear in the pages of these guides. The staff is committed to this research. It's dirty work, but we're glad to do it for you.

The illustrations and maps in these books are the work of Harry Teel and Pete Chadwell. As a fly fisherman, Pete is more than happy to apply his considerable drawing talents to things that live and float in and on water. His detailed maps are a testimony to his desire for accuracy and to get out and fly fish new waters.

The computer work and design of No Nonsense guides is the work of Aprille Chadwell. Aprille's firm, Dynamic Arts, provides graphic art services for a variety of clients. She was dragged into producing No Nonsense fly fishing guides by the publisher and her husband.

Look for new No Nonsense Fly Fishing guides to other important regions!

OREGON
HIGHWAY MAP

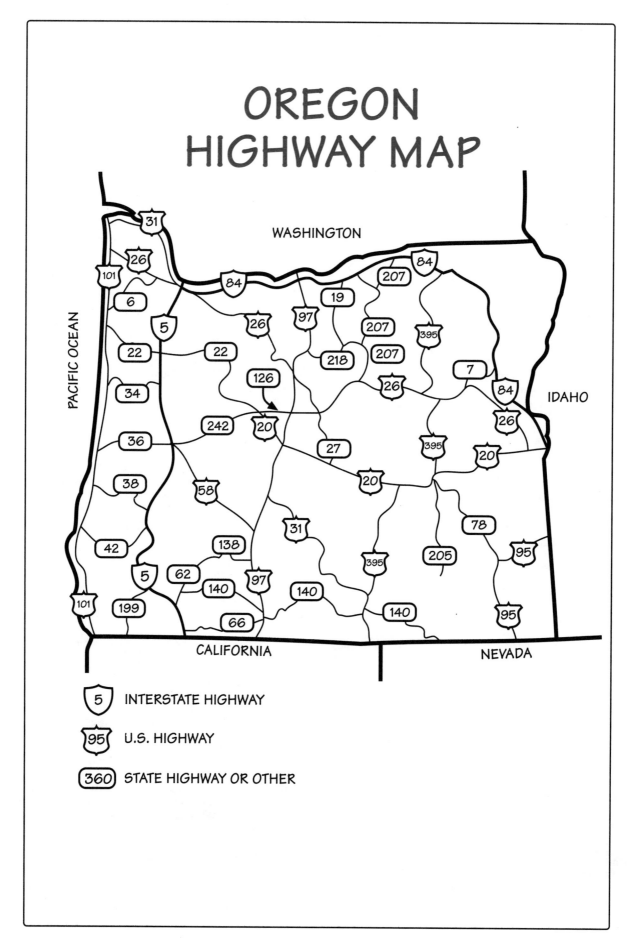

WASHINGTON

PACIFIC OCEAN

IDAHO

CALIFORNIA

NEVADA

5 INTERSTATE HIGHWAY

95 U.S. HIGHWAY

360 STATE HIGHWAY OR OTHER